Mit unseren Begleitmaterialien zu English Network zu optimalen Lernerfolgen

Unsere Lernercassetten bzw. -CDs enthalten alle mit **weißem** Cassettensymbol gekennzeichneten Dialoge (mit Nachsprechpausen!) sowie Ausspracheübungen aus den jeweiligen Lektionsteilen.

Unsere Textcassetten bzw. -CDs enthalten Hörtexte, die für den Gruppenunterricht mit Kursleiter/in gedacht sind; ein **schwarzes** Cassettensymbol weist auf solche Texte hin. Wenn Sie diese T... 'ause nacharbeiten möchten, dann empfiehlt sich die Anschaffung.

Unser Wiederholungsheft Break frischt erworbene Kennt... unterrichtsfreien Zeit wieder auf – Sie sind für den neuen Kursbeginn dann b...

W0241421

Ich bestelle hiermit:

English Network Starter

O **Lernercassette 1 (Units 1–3)**
(Best.-Nr. 3-526-**57 561**-4 / DM 17,90* / öS 132,–* / sFr. 17,00*)

O **Lernercassette 2** (Units 4–6)
(Best.-Nr. 3-526-**57 562**-2 / DM 17,90* / öS 132,–* / sFr. 17,00*)

O **Lerner-CD 1 (Units 1–3)**
(Best.-Nr. 3-526-**57 550**-9 / DM 19,80* / öS 147,–* / sFr. 19,00*)

O **Lerner-CD 2 (Units 4–6)**
(Best.-Nr. 3-526-**57 551**-7 / DM 19,80* / öS 147,–* / sFr. 19,00*)

O **2 Textcassetten (Units 1–6)** – Institutsversion –
(Best.-Nr. 3-526-**57 560**-6 / DM 39,80* / öS 295,–* / sFr. 37,00*)

O **2 Text-CDs (Units 1–6)** – Institutsversion –
(Best.-Nr. 3-526-**57 519**-3 / DM 39,80* / öS 295,–* / sFr. 37,00*)

O **Break 1 (Wiederholungsheft)**
(Best.-Nr. 3-526-**50 393**-1 / DM 10,90* / öS 80,–* / sFr. 10,50*)

Unterschrift/Datum (Absender auf Vorderseite ---->)

* Preisänderung vorbehalten
\- Zutreffendes ist angekreuzt -

Ich bestelle hiermit:

English Network Starter

O **Lernercassette 1 (Units 1–3)**
(Best.-Nr. 3-526-**57 561**-4 / DM 17,90* / öS 132,–* / sFr. 17,00*)

O **Lernercassette 2** (Units 4–6)
(Best.-Nr. 3-526-**57 562**-2 / DM 17,90* / öS 132,–* / sFr. 17,00*)

O **Lerner-CD 1 (Units 1–3)**
(Best.-Nr. 3-526-**57 550**-9 / DM 19,80* / öS 147,–* / sFr. 19,00*)

O **Lerner-CD 2 (Units 4–6)**
(Best.-Nr. 3-526-**57 551**-7 / DM 19,80* / öS 147,–* / sFr. 19,00*)

O **2 Textcassetten (Units 1–6)** – Institutsversion –
(Best.-Nr. 3-526-**57 560**-6 / DM 39,80* / öS 295,–* / sFr. 37,00*)

O **2 Text-CDs (Units 1–6)** – Institutsversion –
(Best.-Nr. 3-526-**57 519**-3 / DM 39,80* / öS 295,–* / sFr. 37,00*)

O **Break 1 (Wiederholungsheft)**
(Best.-Nr. 3-526-**50 393**-1 / DM 10,90* / öS 80,–* / sFr. 10,50*)

Unterschrift/Datum (Absender auf Vorderseite ---->)

* Preisänderung vorbehalten
\- Zutreffendes ist angekreuzt -

Absender:

___
Name/Vorname

___
Straße/Nr.

___
PLZ/Ort

Bitte liefern Sie die angekreuzten Titel über die Buchhandlung

___
Name/Straße

___
PLZ/Ort

(Sollte keine Buchhandlung genannt sein, erfolgt die Lieferung über eine Buchhandlung nach Wahl des Verlags.)

Antwort

An den Verlag
Langenscheidt-Longman
Postfach 40 11 20

80711 München

ENGLISH network STARTER

Michele Charlton, Nicola Karásek
und Carolyn Kilday Wittmann
mit
Ingrid Boczkowski und Dieter Kranz

Langenscheidt-Longman
ENGLISH LANGUAGE TEACHING

English Network Starter

Lehrwerkskomponenten:	
Kursbuch	50 390
Textcassetten	57 560
Text-CDs	57 519
Lernercassette 1	57 561
Lernercassette 2	57 562
Lerner-CD 1	57 550
Lerner-CD 2	57 551
Lehrerhandreichungen	50 391
Break	50 393
Einstufungstest	50 392

Autoren:
Michele Charlton, Nicola Karásek,
Carolyn Kilday Wittmann (Unitteil),
Ingrid Boczkowski
(Revision and Extension und Extra)
Dr. Dieter Kranz (Grammatik)

Beratende Mitwirkung:
Dr. Donald Porsché

Projektteam:
Prof. Dr. Jürgen Beneke, Consultant für betrieblichen Fremdsprachen-
unterricht und Unternehmenskommunikation, Hildesheim
Ingrid Boczkowski, Fachbereichsleiterin, Völklingen
Michele Charlton, Kursleiterin, Genf
Nicola Karásek, Kursleiterin und Lehrbeauftragte, München
Carolyn Kilday Wittmann, Kursleiterin und Lehrbeauftragte, München
Peter Kirchhoff, Fachbereichsleiter, Wuppertal
Dr. Dieter Kranz, Kursleiter und Akademischer Direktor, Münster
Gerry Montague, Volkshochschulleiter, Burghausen
Dr. Donald Porsché, Programmbereichsleiter, Frankfurt
Gaynor Ramsey, Autorin, Kursleiterin und Lehrerfortbildnerin, Zürich
Michael Rutman, Landesbeauftragter, Zürich
Silvia Stephan, Kursleiterin und Lehrerfortbildnerin, Offenburg

Verlagsredaktion:
John Stevens, Projektleiter
Doris Michels, Redakteurin

Design:
Sylvia Tate

Illustrationen:
Terry Gabbey
John Fraser

Auftragsphotos:
Trevor Clifford

Graphik und Layout:
Christine Rechl, Jürgen Bartz

Umschlag:
Zero Grafik & Design GmbH

Umschlagphoto: Cottages am Fluß Severn in Tewkesbury, Gloucestershire.

Umwelthinweis: Gedruckt auf chlorfrei gebleichtem Papier.

1. Auflage 1991

Druck: Mateu Cromo, S.A. Pinto (Madrid).
Printed in Spain
ISBN 3-526-50390-7

15 16 17/02 01 00

Wegweiser

Hier geben wir Ihnen einen kurzen Überblick über das, was Sie von diesem Englischkurs erwarten dürfen, sowie einige Informationen, die Ihnen helfen, sich im Buch zurechtzufinden.

Für wen ist das Buch gedacht?

English Network Starter wendet sich an alle Erwachsenen, die zum allerersten Mal Englisch lernen. Es werden keinerlei Vorkenntnisse vorausgesetzt. Sie beginnen bei Punkt Null und schaffen sich eine solide Basis von Sprachkenntnissen, auf die Sie später, wenn Sie möchten, weiter aufbauen können.

Was lerne ich?

In diesem Buch begleiten Sie Tina und Mark aus Hamburg auf einer Urlaubsreise nach England. Die beiden kommen als Urlauber in Situationen, in denen sie sich anderen vorstellen, Freunde begrüßen, sich erkundigen, nach dem Weg fragen, Ausflüge machen und darüber berichten. So lernen Sie die Redewendungen, die Sie brauchen, um sich in den wichtigsten Situationen mit Englisch sprechenden Menschen unterhalten zu können. Das kann im Ausland sein, aber genausogut zu Hause in der Heimat, wenn Sie hier Ausländern begegnen. Am Ende des Buches kennen Sie bereits über 300 englische Wörter, können Fragen stellen und beantworten und über die Gegenwart und die Vergangenheit sprechen. Sie können Gespräche führen und einfache Texte verstehen.

Wie lerne ich?

Mit *English Network* lernen Sie nicht allein, sondern in einer Gruppe mit anderen Kursteilnehmern und -teilnehmerinnen. Alle haben die gleiche Ausgangsbasis wie Sie und ähnliche Ziele. Sie hören Cassetten, üben das Sprechen, lesen Dialoge und Texte und schreiben Sätze oder kurze Texte über sich auf. Sie arbeiten mal alle zusammen, mal alleine, mal mit einem anderen Kursmitglied oder einer kleinen Gruppe von Kursmitgliedern zusammen. Ihr Kursleiter / Ihre Kursleiterin weiß, wie mit dem Buch unterrichtet wird, und steht Ihnen mit Rat und Tat zur Seite. In jedem Kapitel des Buches finden Sie außerdem Lerntips, die Ihnen helfen, besser und schneller zu lernen. Mit Hilfe der Lernercassetten und dem *Homestudy*-Teil können Sie Ihre fremdsprachlichen Fähigkeiten auch alleine vertiefen.

Wie ist das Buch aufgebaut?

Das Buch besteht aus einer fortlaufenden Geschichte, die in 6 Units, d.h. Lerneinheiten, eingeteilt ist. Jede Unit bildet ein Kapitel in der Geschichte von Mark und Tinas Urlaubsreise.
Die Units bearbeiten Sie mit Ihrem Kursleiter / Ihrer Kursleiterin. Die *Homestudy*-Seiten mit zusätzlichen Übungen sind für die Nacharbeit zu Hause gedacht. Wenn Sie Ihren Lernerfolg absichern wollen, sollten Sie versuchen, diese Seiten regelmäßig miteinzuplanen.
Im Anhang des Buches finden Sie Informationen, die Ihnen beim Lernen helfen. Zunächst finden Sie den Schlüssel zu den *Homestudy*-Übungen. Unter der Rubrik *Andere Länder, andere Sitten* stehen dann nützliche Hintergrundinformationen über das Leben in Großbritannien. Dem Wortschatzlernen und -nachschlagen dienen *Vocabulary* und *Dictionary*, die den gesamten Wortschatz des Buches mit Beispielen und deutscher Übersetzung auflisten. Außerdem bietet der Anhang einen *Leitfaden Aussprache* und eine *Student-Check List*, aus der Sie ersehen können, was Sie alles gelernt haben und wie sich Ihre Englischkenntnisse von Unit zu Unit aufbauen. Auf der Umschlaginnenseite (hinten) gibt es schließlich eine Auflistung häufiger Übungsanweisungen zum schnellen Nachschlagen.

Bevor es nun mit Unit 1 richtig losgeht, finden Sie auf den nächsten sechs Seiten einen *Starter*, der den Einstieg in die Arbeit mit dem Buch erleichtern soll.

Viel Spaß und viel Erfolg beim Lernen
wünschen Ihnen

Autorenteam und Verlag

Übrigens: Wenn Sie in den Sommerferien Ihre Kenntnisse festigen möchten, können Sie mit ***English Network Starter Break*** auf unterhaltsame Weise Grammatik, Wortschatz und Redewendungen aus dem Kursbuch wiederholen. Damit sind Sie für das neue Semester bestens vorbereitet!

Diese Symbole kennzeichnen alle Teile, zu denen Tonaufnahmen vorliegen. Die Textcassetten enthalten sämtliche Aufnahmen. Die Lernercassetten enthalten die Dialoge mit Pausen zum Nachsprechen und die Übungen *Listen and repeat* aus *Listening and pronunciation.*
Die Lernercassetten sind auch als CDs erhältlich.

Starter

1

2

3

4

5

6

7

8

9

10

11

12

13

14

15

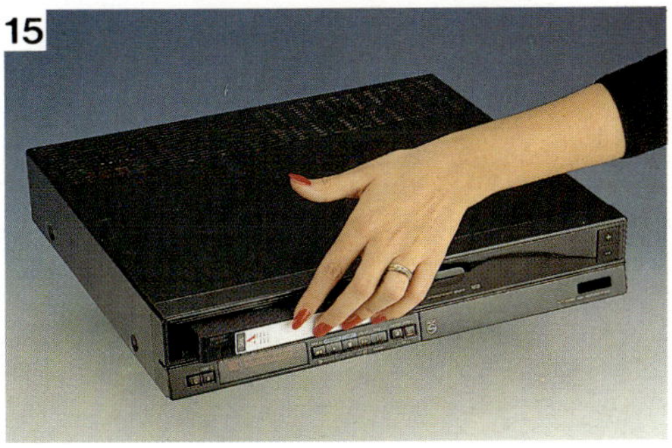

Sie können noch kein Englisch? Doch bestimmt. Es gibt eine Menge Wörter, die im Englischen und im Deutschen gleich oder fast gleich sind. Sicher kennen Sie welche. Schauen Sie sich die Fotos an und versuchen Sie, die folgenden Wörter den Fotos zuzuordnen.

a. computer	i. sandwich
b. tennis	j. hamburger
c. hotel	k. park
d. T-shirt	l. jeans
e. mountain bike	m. steak
f. squash	n. sweatshirt
g. video	o. golf
h. bank	

In welche Gruppen können die Wörter zusammengefaßt werden: Kleidung? Sport? ... ?

Kennen Sie noch weitere Wörter?

Die Personen

Tina and Mark from Hamburg

In diesem Buch begleiten Sie Tina und Mark aus Hamburg auf einer Urlaubsreise nach England. Mark arbeitet bei der Bundesbahn und lernt seit zwei Jahren Englisch an der Volkshochschule. Tina, gebürtige Engländerin, arbeitet als Sekretärin bei einer großen internationalen Firma in Hamburg.

Tina stammt aus King's Lynn, einer kleinen Stadt in Ostengland, etwa 150 Kilometer von London. Ihre Schwester Karen lebt noch dort. Karen macht z.Zt. Urlaub und hat Tina und Mark solange ihr Haus überlassen. Tina und Mark machen also für einige Wochen "Haussitting" in King's Lynn, so wie andere Babysitting machen.

Karen's house

Die Nachbarin in King's Lynn heißt Helen Kemp. Helen unterhält eine *Bed-and-Breakfast*-Unterkunft, d.h. sie vermietet Zimmer mit Frühstück an Reisende und Feriengäste. Bei Helen ist der Schlüssel zu Karens Haus hinterlegt. Und auch sonst steht sie den Besuchern aus Hamburg hilfreich zur Seite.

Helen Kemp

Norman Kemp

Helen ist mit Norman verheiratet, der als Automechaniker arbeitet. Sie haben eine Tochter Vanessa, eine pfiffige Teenagerin, die noch zur Schule geht. Helen und Normans Sohn John ist bereits erwachsen. Er arbeitet bei einer Bank.

John Kemp

Vanessa Kemp

Mr and Mrs Wilson

Ferner werden Sie – mit Tina und Mark – in King's Lynn kennenlernen: Mr und Mrs Wilson, Rentnerehepaar und ebenfalls Nachbarn, sowie Chris, einen amerikanischen Freund Johns, der bei der britischen Filiale einer amerikanischen Computerfirma arbeitet.

John's American friend Chris

DER INHALT

Arrival

King's Lynn
Norfolk

Population: 46 000

London: 150 km

Cambridge: 70 km

Norwich: 70 km

Unit 1

Ankunft in King's Lynn. Tina und Mark lernen die Familie Kemp kennen und holen den Schlüssel für ihre Ferienunterkunft ab. In dieser Unit lernen Sie u.a.:

- sich vorstellen
- andere begrüßen
- eine Einladung annehmen
- jemandem danken
- sagen und fragen, woher man kommt.

STEP 1

Hello!

STARTER

DIALOGUE

Part 1

Helen: Hello, Tina.
Tina: Hello, Helen.

Vanessa: Hello. I'm Vanessa.
Mark: Hello, Vanessa. I'm Mark.

Part 2

Helen: How are you?
Tina: I'm fine, thanks. And how are you?
Helen: Fine, thanks.

Part 3

Tina: Helen, this is Mark.
Mark, this is Helen.
Mark: Hello, Helen.
Helen: Hello, Mark. Nice to meet you.

ACTIVITIES

Part 1

1a And now you.

Begrüßen Sie einige Mitglieder Ihres Englischkurses und stellen Sie sich ihnen vor.

Example:
A: Hello, I'm (Silvia Braun).
B: Hello, I'm (Hans Jung).

Part 2

2a Please complete.

Bitte setzen Sie die richtigen Wörter in die Lücken ein.

2b And now you.

Fragen Sie einige Kursmitglieder, wie es ihnen geht.

Example:
A: Hello, (Silvia). How are you?
B: I'm fine, thanks and how are you?
A: Fine, thanks.

Part 3

3a What's the right order?

Ordnen Sie die Wörter, so daß sie Sätze ergeben.

Tina: Mark / is / Helen / this.
Mark: Helen / nice / hello / meet / to / you.
Helen: to / Mark / hello / you / nice / meet.

3b And now you.

Bilden Sie mit zwei anderen Kursmitgliedern eine Gruppe zu dritt. Stellen Sie sich gegenseitig vor. (→ *Andere Länder, andere Sitten*)

Example:
A: (Silvia), this is (Hans). (Hans), this is (Silvia).
B: Hello, (Hans).
C: Hello, (Silvia). Nice to meet you.

Stellen Sie nun ein Mitglied Ihrer Gruppe der Klasse vor: This is (Hans).

Listening & pronunciation

4a Listen again.

Schließen Sie Ihr Buch und hören Sie jetzt den Dialog von Seite 12 nochmals komplett an.

4b Listen and repeat.

How are you?
I'm fine, thanks.

Helen, this is Mark.
Hello, Mark. Nice to meet you.

4c Listen and match.

Schauen Sie sich zunächst die Bilder an und hören Sie dann drei Gespräche auf der Cassette. Welcher Dialog paßt zu welchem Bild?

GRAMMAR

1 Wie Sie jemanden begrüßen:

Hello	Guten Tag / Hallo

2 Wie Sie sich jemandem vorstellen:

I'm (= I am) ...	Ich bin ... / Ich heiße ...

3 Wie Sie auf eine solche Vorstellung reagieren:

Nice to meet you.	Nett, Sie/Dich kennenzulernen.

4 Wie Sie jemanden einer dritten Person vorstellen:

(Silvia), **this is** (Hans).	(Silvia), dies/das ist (Hans).

5 Wie Sie sich nach dem Befinden einer Person erkundigen:

How are you?	Wie geht es Ihnen/Dir?

6 Wie Sie auf eine solche Frage reagieren können:

I'm fine, thanks.	Mir geht es gut, danke.
Fine, thanks.	Gut, danke.

7 Wie Sie *am/are/is* verwenden:

Mit den Ausdrücken oben haben Sie einige wichtige Formeln kennengelernt, die es Ihnen ermöglichen, Kontakte auf Englisch zu fremden Personen zu knüpfen. In den Beispielsätzen spielen die Verbformen *am/are/is* eine wichtige Rolle.

I am / I'm ...	Ich bin ...
You are / You're ...	Du bist / Sie sind ...
This is ...	Dies ist ...

Sie sehen, daß neben den Langformen *am* und *are* auch die Kurzformen *'m* und *'re* verwendet werden. Dies geschieht besonders beim Sprechen.

1 Please complete: is/are/am.

1 I ..... fine.
2 You ..... fine.
3 This ..... fine.

2 Please complete: I or you?

1 John: How are .....?
2 Mary: .....'m fine, thanks.
How are .....?
3 John: .....'m fine.
4 John: This is Peter.
Peter: Nice to meet ..... .

3 Please complete.

Vervollständigen Sie den Satz. Hier sind die fehlenden Buchstaben:
e - e - e - e - i - o - o - o - u

H_ll_. N_c_ t_ m_ _t y_ _.

HOMESTUDY

Lerntip

Machen Sie aus jeder Kursstunde das Beste, denn die Zeit, die Sie im Gruppenunterricht mit Ihrem Kursleiter / Ihrer Kursleiterin verbringen, ist ja begrenzt. Arbeiten Sie aktiv mit, trauen Sie sich, haben Sie keine Angst vor Fehlern; sie gehören zum Lernen dazu. Wenn Sie etwas nicht verstehen, scheuen Sie sich nicht, Ihren Kursleiter / Ihre Kursleiterin zu fragen.

1 Please complete.

hello are this hello nice meet fine is

Jane: Hello Robert. How ..... you?
Robert: ..... Jane. I'm ....., thanks.
Jane, ... is Sarah.
Sarah, this ..... Jane.
Sarah: ..... Jane. ..... to ..... you.

2 Crossword

Setzen Sie die richtigen Wörter in den Dialog ein und schreiben Sie sie dann in das Kreuzworträtsel. Wie heißt das Lösungswort?

Norman: Steve, ..(1).. is Tina.
Steve: ..(2).. Tina. How ..(3).. you?
Tina: I'm ..(4).., thanks. And you?
Steve: Fine, ..(5)...
Tina: Steve, this ..(6).. Mark.
Steve: Hello, Mark. Nice to meet you.

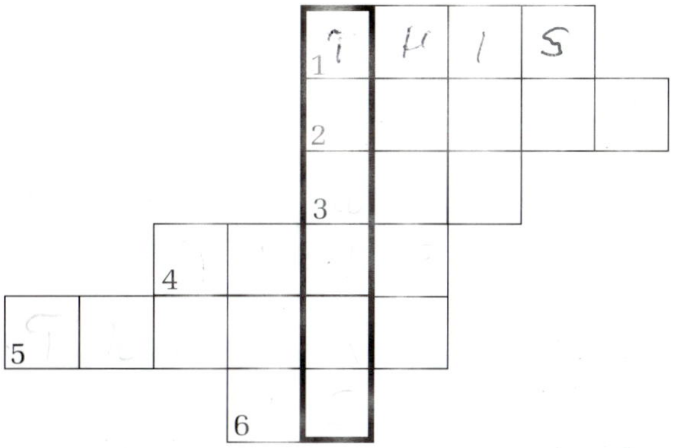

3 Please match.

1 Hello.
2 How are you?
3 I'm Robert.

☐ a Nice to meet you.
1 b Hello.
☐ c I'm fine, thanks.

Example: 1 Hello. b Hello.

4 Say it in English: please match.

1 Sie begrüßen jemanden.
2 Sie stellen Tina einer anderen Person vor.
3 Sie fragen jemanden, wie es ihm geht.
4 Sie sind erfreut, eine andere Person kennenzulernen.
5 Sie sagen, daß es Ihnen gut geht.

☐ a How are you?
☐ b Nice to meet you.
1 c Hello.
☐ d I'm fine, thanks.
☐ e This is Tina.

STEP 2

Come in, please

STARTER

1 Revision

Stellen Sie sich anderen Kursmitgliedern vor und fragen Sie, wie es ihnen geht.
Stellen Sie nun Ihren Nachbarn oder Ihre Nachbarin den anderen Kursmitgliedern vor.

2 Vocabulary

Listen and repeat: a cup of tea, a cup of coffee, a hamburger, a sandwich, an orange, an apple, a banana, a biscuit, an ice-cream.

DIALOGUE

Part 1

Helen: Come in, please.
Tina: Thanks.
Helen: Mark, have a seat.
Mark: Thank you.

Part 2

Helen: Mark, a cup of tea?
Mark: Yes, please.
Helen: And a biscuit?
Mark: No, thank you.
Helen: Tina, and you? A cup of tea and a biscuit?
Tina: Yes, please.
Helen: Vanessa, a biscuit?
Vanessa: No thanks, Mum. An ice-cream, please.
(→ *Andere Länder, andere Sitten*)

Part 3

Norman: Hello. You must be Mark.
Mark: Yes, I am. And you must be Norman.
Norman: Yes, I am. Welcome to King's Lynn, Mark.
Mark: Thank you. Nice to meet you, Norman.

ACTIVITIES

Part 1

1a And now you.

Fünf Kursmitglieder verlassen bitte das Klassenzimmer, die übrigen bitten sie nacheinander wieder herein.

Part 2

2a And now you.

Sie sind auf einem Fest. Bieten Sie Ihrem Nachbarn / Ihrer Nachbarin Speisen und Getränke aus *Vocabulary* (S.16) an.
Example:
A: An ice-cream, (Silvia)?
B: No, thanks.
A: A sandwich?
B: Yes, please.

Part 3

3a And now you.

Bitten Sie Ihren Kursleiter oder Ihre Kursleiterin um die Teilnehmerliste. Sprechen Sie mit Hilfe der Liste ein anderes Kursmitglied an und geben Sie die Liste dann an diese Person weiter.
Example:
A: You must be (Silvia Braun).
B: Yes, I am. I'm Silvia Braun. *or:*
No, I'm Anita Kahl.
A: Nice to meet you, Silvia/Anita.

3b Please complete.

1 Welcome to King's Lynn.
2 Welcome to N... Y.... .
3 W...... t...... P....... .
4 .... to L......... .
5 (Your town)

Listening & pronunciation

4a Listen again.

Listen to the dialogue parts 1-3 again.

4b Listen and repeat.

Helen erwartet einen kanadischen Freund ihrer Schwester als Pensionsgast. Hören Sie den Begrüßungsdialog und sprechen Sie die Sätze von Helen nach.

Helen: Hello, you must be Tom.
Tom: And you must be Helen.
Helen: Welcome to King's Lynn.
Tom: Thank you. Nice to meet you.
Helen: How are you?
Tom: I'm fine, thank you. And you?
Helen: Fine, thanks. Please come in.
Tom: Thank you, Helen.

4c Listen and complete.

Vanessas Schulkameradinnen Mary, Janet und Kate sind zu Besuch. Hören Sie im Dialog, was Helen ihnen anbietet und kreuzen Sie in der Übersicht an, was Janet und Vanessa haben möchten.

				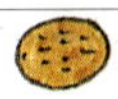
Kate				
Janet				
Mary				
Vanessa				

GRAMMAR

1 Wie Sie jemanden zu etwas auffordern:

Come in.	Komm herein / Kommen Sie herein.
Have a seat.	Setz Dich / Setzen Sie sich.

2 Und so wird man sich bei Ihnen bedanken:

Thank you.	Vielen Dank.
Thanks.	Danke.

3 Wie Sie etwas anbieten:

A cup of tea?	Eine Tasse Tee?
A biscuit?	Ein Plätzchen? / Möchtest Du / Möchten Sie ein Plätzchen?

4 Ein solches Angebot können Sie entweder dankend annehmen oder ablehnen:

Yes, please.	Ja bitte.
No, thank you. / No, thanks.	Nein, vielen Dank.

5 Vermutungen können mit *must* ausgedrückt werden:

You **must be** Mark.	Du mußt / Sie müssen Mark sein.

6 Der unbestimmte Artikel *a/an:*

a cup of tea	eine Tasse Tee
a biscuit	ein Plätzchen

Das Wort *a* verändert sich nicht, bis auf eine Ausnahme: Vor einem Selbstlaut (a, e, i, o, u) heißt der unbestimmte Artikel *an*. Dadurch können Sie die Wörter in ihrer Abfolge leichter aussprechen und aneinander binden.

1 Who is it?

Wer ist das? Erkennen Sie diese Personen?
Example: This must be ...

2 Please complete: a or an?

1 ... seat
2 ... cup of tea
3 ... orange
4 ... ice-cream
5 ... biscuit
6 ... apple

3 Please complete this dialogue.

A: Come ....., ... a seat.
B: ..... you.
A: A cup of tea?
B: Yes, ...
A: A biscuit?
B: No, ...

HOMESTUDY

Lerntip

Zwischen einer Kursstunde und der nächsten liegt meist soviel Zeit, daß ein Teil des Gelernten wieder vergessen wird. Das muß aber nicht sein, weil Sie mit einfachen Mitteln zuhause oder unterwegs den Lernerfolg absichern können. Sie können den Stoff der letzten Kursstunde wiederholen, die Übungen auf dieser Seite bearbeiten (sie sind extra für die Arbeit zuhause gedacht), nützliche Redewendungen auswendig lernen. Aber nicht alles auf einmal. Das Motto heißt: lieber wenig, dafür öfter. Zehn Minuten jeden Tag bringen mehr als einmal die Woche zwei Stunden.

1 Please complete: a or an?

1 A cup of tea, please.
2 ... orange, please.
3 ...
4 ...
5 ...

2 What's the right order?

Helen: tea/Have/of/cup/a
Mark: you/Thank.
Helen: biscuit/And/a?
Mark: thanks/No.

3 Please match and make words.

Welche Buchstaben passen zusammen? Ordnen Sie sie so, daß Sie 6 Wörter erhalten.

Example: 1f = must

1 mu	☐ a come
2 tha	☐ b cuit
3 ple	☐ c nks
4 ice	☐ d ase
5 bis	☐ e cream
6 wel	☐ f st

4 Say it in English: please match.

1 Sie bitten jemanden Platz zu nehmen.
2 Sie heißen jemanden in King's Lynn willkommen.
3 Sie bieten eine Tasse Tee an.
4 Sie vermuten, daß jemand John ist.
5 Sie bitten jemanden herein.

[2] a Welcome to King's Lynn.
[3] b Have a cup of tea.
[5] c Come in, please.
[4] d You must be John.
[1] e Have a seat.

STEP 3

Where are you from?

STARTER

1 Revision

Look at the pictures. Who is it? Example: This must be ...

2 Vocabulary

1	2	3	4	5	6	7	8	9	10
one	two	three	four	five	six	seven	eight	nine	ten

DIALOGUE

Part 1

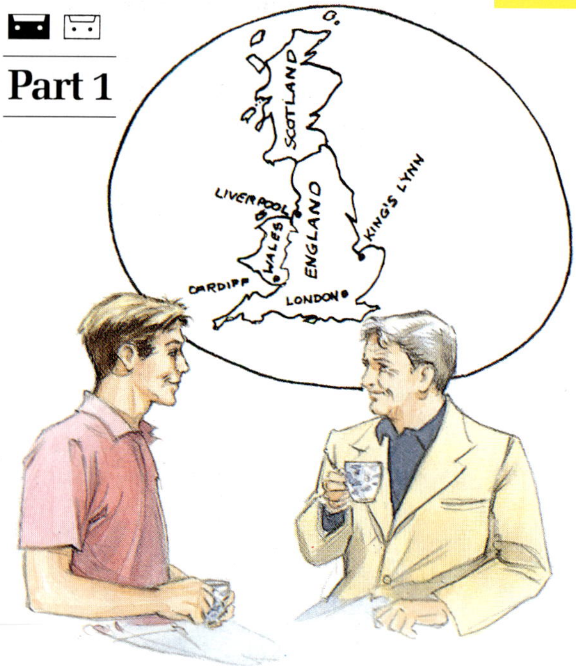

Norman: Mark, where are you from in Germany?
Mark: I'm from Hamburg.
Norman: Oh, yes.
Mark: Where are you from? Are you from King's Lynn?
Norman: No, I'm not. I'm from Wales.
(→ *Andere Länder, andere Sitten*)

Part 2

Vanessa: He's from Cardiff.
Mark: And Helen? Is she from Cardiff, too?
Vanessa: No, she isn't. She's from Liverpool. But I'm from King's Lynn.

Part 3

Helen: Tina, here's the key for number 8.
Tina: Oh, yes, thank you. And thank you for the tea.
Helen: You're welcome. Oh, the phone ... . 327094. Hello? (→ *Andere Länder, andere Sitten*)

ACTIVITIES

Part 1

1a And now you.

Ask four students in the class. Example:
A: Where are you from?
B: I'm from ...

1b Are you from King's Lynn?

Wählen Sie eine Stadt, in der Sie gerne wohnen möchten: Paris, Amsterdam, King's Lynn, New York, London, Rimini, Berlin oder Lugano. Die anderen Kursmitglieder sollen Ihre Stadt erraten.
Example:
A: Are you from King's Lynn?
B: No, I'm not.
C: Are you from ...?

Part 2

2a This is ...

Introduce your partner to the class. Examples:

– This is Heinz. He's from Salzburg in Austria.
– This is Doris. She's from Lugano in Switzerland.
– This is Anna. She's from Ulm in Germany.

2b Memory game

Now ask your partner about the class. Example:
A: Where's (Heinz/Doris/Anna/...) from?
B: He's/She's from ... in ... .

Part 3

3a Thank you.

Example:
A: Thank you for the biscuit.
B: You're welcome.

3b Phone numbers

Listen and repeat.

1. 520693 2. 202158 3. 335278

Now say the numbers.

1. 364783 2. 918327 3. 463592
4. 965507 5. 236419

And now you. Ask your partner.
A: What's your phone number?
B: It's ...

Listening & pronunciation

4a Listen again.

Listen to the dialogue parts 1-3 again.

4b Listen. The same or different?

Sie hören jeweils drei Wörter. Wird der Buchstabe 'o' in ihnen gleich (*the same*) oder verschieden (*different*) ausgesprochen? Streichen Sie die richtige Lösung an.

				the same	different
1	oh	no	hello		
2	ok	how	from		
3	no	ok	hello		
4	not	from	of		
5	to	or	no		

4c Listen and write the numbers.

Example:
Cassette: 'Two and two is ...'
You write: 2 + 2 =

1 2+2 =
2 ...
3 ...
4 ...
5 ...
6 ...
7 ...
8 ...

Now say the answer. Example:
1 Two and two is four.
2 ...

GRAMMAR

1 Wie Sie fragen, wo jemand herkommt und darauf antworten:

Where are you from?	Wo kommst Du / kommen Sie her?
I'm from ...	Ich bin aus ...

2 Aussagen mit *am/are/is* (das Verb *to be*):

I'm / I am from London.	Ich bin ...
You're/ You are from Berlin.	Du bist / Sie sind ...
He's / He is from Germany.	Er ist ...
She's / She is from Austria.	Sie ist ...
This is Hans.	Dies ist ...

'm/'re/'s sind Kurzformen von *am/are/is* und werden beim Sprechen verwendet.

3 Fragen mit *are/is:*

Die englische Frage mit *are/is*, auf die man mit 'Ja' oder 'Nein' antworten kann, wird wie im Deutschen gebildet.

Are you from King's Lynn?	Bist Du / Sind Sie aus King's Lynn?
Is he/she from Germany?	Kommt/Ist er/sie aus Deutschland?

Auf solche Fragen gibt man sogenannte "Kurzantworten".

4 Kurzantworten mit *am/are/is:*

Bejaht: mit Langform	Verneint: mit Kurzform
Yes, I am.	**No, I'm not.**
Yes, you are.	**No, you aren't.**
Yes, he/she is.	**No, he/she isn't.**

5 Fragen mit Fragewort:

Um etwas zu erfahren, z.B. woher jemand kommt, werden Fragen gebildet, die mit einem Fragewort beginnen.

Where are you **from?**	Woher kommst Du / kommen Sie?
Where is she **from?**	Woher kommt sie?

Diese Fragen können nicht mit 'Ja' oder 'Nein' beantwortet werden, da eine Information verlangt wird. Sie könnte auf die gestellten Fragen lauten: *I'm from Hamburg* und *She's from Liverpool.*

1 Please complete: 'm – 'm not – is – 's – isn't – are

N: Hello, I..... Nick Jones.
H: Hello, I..... Hans Maier.
N: You must be from Germany.
H: No, I..... .
N: Oh, you aren't from Germany! Where ..... you from?
H: From Austria. I..... from Salzburg, but Maria..... from Germany.
N: ..... she from Berlin?
H: No, she ..... . She..... from Leipzig.

2 Write the questions.

1 Where ..... from? – I'm from Scotland.
2 ..... from Glasgow? – No, I'm not. I'm from Dundee.
3 And ..... Peter from Scotland? – No, he isn't.
4 Oh, where ..... from? – He's from Wales.
5 Where ..... in Wales? – He's from Cardiff.

3 Write about three students in the class.

Example:
Klaus. He's from Dresden.
He isn't from Munich.
Anna. She's from ...

HOMESTUDY

Lerntip

Arbeiten Sie von Anfang an nicht nur in der gesamten Lerngruppe, sondern auch paarweise oder zu dritt. Dadurch kommen Sie schneller voran, weil Sie mehr reden und intensiver üben können. Sie werden feststellen, daß Sie sich bald gegenseitig helfen können, auch wenn zu Beginn des Kurses keine(r) die geringsten Vorkenntnisse hatte. Wichtig noch: arbeiten Sie nicht immer mit denselben Kursmitgliedern zusammen, sondern mit allen. Das macht flexibel und hilft Ihnen später, sich auf ganz verschiedene Stimmen einzustellen. Und: bemühen Sie sich, die Namen aller anderen Kursmitglieder zu lernen. Das erleichtert vieles.

1 True or false?

Schauen Sie sich den Dialog auf Seite 20 an. Sind die folgenden Aussagen richtig (*true*) oder falsch (*false*)?

	True	False
1 Helen is from King's Lynn.		
2 Norman is from Wales.		
3 Vanessa is from Hamburg.		
4 Norman isn't from King's Lynn.		
5 Mark is from Munich.		

2 Please complete: for – from – in – of – to.

1 Thank you ..... the tea.
2 Welcome ..... King's Lynn.
3 Are you ..... Liverpool?
4 Please come ..... . A cup ..... tea?
5 This is the key ..... number 8.

3 Please match and make questions.

1 Where are you
2 Is she
3 Are you from
4 How are
5 Is this the

☐ a Germany?
☐ b you?
☐ c key?
☐ d from?
☐ e nice?

4 Please complete: is – 's – isn't – am – 'm –are.

Mark: Where ..... you from?
Norman: I ..... from Cardiff.
Mark: ..... Helen from Cardiff?
Norman: No, she ..... . She..... from Liverpool. And you, Mark, ... you from Germany?
Mark: Yes, I ..... . I..... from Hamburg.

5 Words

Welche der folgenden Wörter reimen sich?

for – nine – three – ice – fine – you – four – tea – nice – seat – two – meet.

6 Say it in English. Please match.

1 Sie bedanken sich bei jemandem für einen Keks.
2 Sie überreichen jemandem einen Schlüssel.
3 Sie möchten wissen, woher jemand ist.
4 Jemand bedankt sich bei Ihnen für den Tee. Was antworten Sie?
5 Sie möchten wissen, ob jemand aus England kommt.

☐ a Are you from England?
☐ b You're welcome.
☐ c Where are you from?
☐ d Here's the key.
☐ e Thank you for the biscuit.

A castle in Wales

REVISION AND EXTENSION

• Starter

What is in the picture?

a banana
a ...
...

1 Please complete.

Maxi: Hello, Minnie.
..... are .....?
Minnie: ....., Maxi.
I'm ....., thanks.
..... how ..... you?
Maxi: Fine, ...
Minnie .... Billy.
Billy, ... Minnie.
Billy: ....., Minnie.
Minnie: ....., Billy. ..... to ..... you.

2 And now you.

Bilden Sie Dreiergruppen. Begrüßen Sie sich und fragen Sie, wie es geht. Stellen Sie dann jemanden vor.

3 Please match.

1 Where are you from?
2 What's your phone number?
3 How are you?
4 Are you from Bristol?
5 Where's King's Lynn?
6 A cup of tea?
7 You must be Chris.

☐ a No, I'm not. I'm Victor.
☐ b Yes, I am.
☐ c From England.
☐ d Yes, please.
☐ e Fine, thanks.
☐ f 771955.
☐ g In England.

4 What's the right order?

a OWT – two
b VEESN – ...
c NEIN – ...
d REETH – ...
e THIEG – ...
f EVIF – ...
g ROFU – ...
h XIS – ...
i NOE – ...

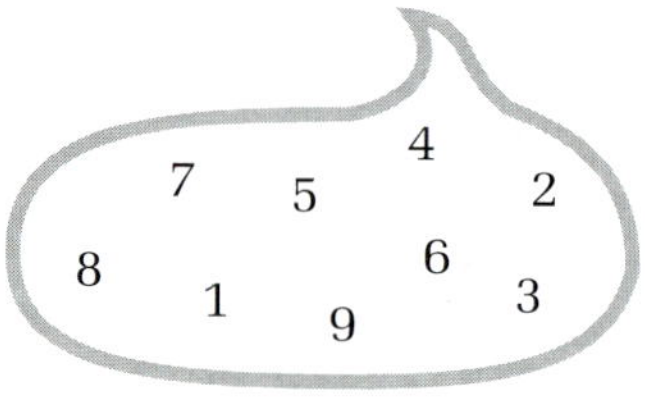

5 Your class list

Start a class list. Ask the students in your class:

Where are you from?
What's your phone number?

NAME	Vera		
FROM	Enkelbach		
PHONE NUMBER	391582		

REVISION AND EXTENSION

6 Find the 10 words.

In diesem Kästchen sind waagerecht 10 Wörter mit vier und mehr Buchstaben versteckt, die Sie in Unit 1 gelernt haben.

Q	O	W	H	E	R	E	Z	E
E	S	E	A	T	Y	O	U	R
M	M	L	E	P	H	O	N	E
N	I	C	E	T	M	E	E	T
F	R	O	M	S	F	I	N	E
C	O	M	E	V	I	T	U	I
P	L	E	A	S	E	C	O	V

Ein 11. Wort finden Sie senkrecht. Hier eine kleine Hilfe:

_ _ _ _ o _ _

7 Memory check

Welche anderen Wörter fallen Ihnen spontan ein, die Sie in Unit 1 gelernt haben? Schreiben Sie sie auf und vergleichen Sie Ihre Liste mit der Ihres Nachbarn / Ihrer Nachbarin.

8 Reading

Hello, I'm Vanessa.
I'm from King's Lynn,
in England.
Daddy isn't from King's
Lynn. He's from Cardiff.
Cardiff is in Wales.
I am a teenager
and I am happy.
Oh and ... my phone number is 327094.
Have a nice day!
So long.

VANESSA.

• Useful phrases

In dieser Rubrik finden Sie zusätzliche Redewendungen, die Sie in der Klasse gebrauchen können und die Ihnen auch im Umgang mit Englisch sprechenden Menschen außerhalb der Klasse helfen.

UNIT 2

Settling in

Unit 2

Tina und Mark packen ihre Koffer aus, sehen sich im Haus um und leben sich in ihrer Ferienunterkunft ein. In dieser Unit lernen Sie u. a.:

- sagen und fragen, welche Gegenstände vorhanden sind und welche Dinge man besitzt
- sagen und fragen, was es an einem Ort gibt
- über Familie und Angehörige sprechen.

STEP 1

The house

STARTER

Vocabulary

Nennen Sie Dinge, die man zuhause in der Wohnung haben kann. Jedes Kursmitglied nennt einen Gegenstand: a phone, a video, a cup of tea …

Zuhause kann man auch haben:

a television

a dictionary

a cat

a dog

a photo

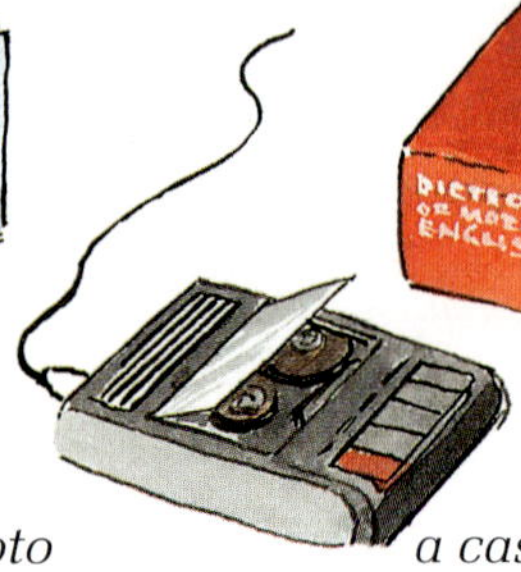

a cassette recorder

DIALOGUE

Part 1

Mark: Have Karen and Paul got a video?
Tina: Yes, they have. And they've got a cassette recorder. For your English cassettes.
Mark: Ha, ha!
Tina: Look, Mark, they've got a photo of Hamburg.
Mark: Really?

Part 2

Mark: I've got a problem …
I haven't got my video camera.
Tina: Never mind.
Mark: Have you got your camera?
Tina: Yes, I have.
Mark: Good.

Part 3

Mark: Have we got the dictionary?
Tina: No, we haven't.
Mark: Oh.
Tina: Never mind, they've got a German – English dictionary here.
Mark: Oh, good.

ACTIVITIES

Part 1

1a What have Karen and Paul got?

Look at part 1 of the dialogue. What have Karen and Paul got? Answer yes (= ✔) or no (= ✘).

	Karen & Paul	Helen & Norman
video		✔
photo of London		✔
computer		✘
television		✔
photo of Hamburg		✘
cassette recorder		✘

Now say what Helen and Norman have got.
Example: They've got a …

Part 2

2a Ask your teacher.

Example: Have you got a cat?
Have you got a ...

2b Please answer: Yes, I have / No, I haven't.

1 Have you got a photo of London?
2 Have you got a television?
3 Have you got a dog?
4 Have you got a camera?
5 Have you got a cassette recorder?
6 Have you got an English cassette?

2c And now you.

Example:
I've got a ... but I haven't got a ...

cat
camera
dog
photo of Hamburg
phone
television
cassette recorder
computer
sweatshirt
video camera
mountain bike

Part 3

3a Exchange information.

Arbeiten Sie mit drei anderen Kursmitgliedern zusammen. Zwei von ihnen sind A und schauen sich diese Seite an. Die anderen sind B und schlagen Seite 112 auf. Stellen Sie sich gegenseitig Fragen, um herauszufinden, was die anderen haben bzw. nicht haben.

A. You are Sam/Sally Cook. In your house you have got:

Ask B questions and answer B's questions.
Example:
A: Have you got a … in your house?
B: Yes, we have. / No, we haven't.

OK? Now tell B what you haven't got:
You've got ... in your house but we haven't got ...
(→ *Andere Länder, andere Sitten*)

Listening & pronunciation

4a Listen again.

Listen to the dialogue parts 1-3 again.

4b Listen and repeat: [f] and [v]

1 **c**o**ff**ee – cup **o**f tea
2 **ph**oto – **v**ideo
3 **f**ine – ne**v**er mind
4 I'm **f**rom Germany – I'**ve** got a camera

4c Listen and complete.

Mr Wilson and Norman are at Norman's house.
What has Norman got?
Yes = ✔, No = ✘.

phone		video	
television		video camera	
photo		cassette	

GRAMMAR

1 Wie Sie ausdrücken, daß Sie etwas haben oder nicht haben mit *have got:*

Dem deutschen Wort 'haben' entspricht das englische *have got.*

I have got / I've got a problem.	Ich habe ein Problem.
They have got / They've got a camera.	Sie haben eine Kamera.

Verneint wird dieser englische Satz, indem an den ersten Teil des Verbs, also an *have*, *n't* (Kurzform von *not*) angehängt wird:

I haven't got a video camera.	Ich habe keine ...
They **haven't got** a photo of Hamburg.	Sie haben kein ...

Warum *have got* und nicht einfach *have*? Dafür gibt es (wie für viele Kleinigkeiten in allen Sprachen) keine eindeutige Erklärung, *got* gehört einfach dazu.

2 *Have got* in Fragesätzen:

Have they got a German dictionary?	Haben sie ein deutsches Wörterbuch?
Have you got a television?	Hast Du / Haben Sie ein Fernsehgerät?

3 Wie Sie auf eine Nachricht reagieren können:

They've got a dictionary here.

– **Really?**	– Wirklich?
– **Good.**	– Gut.
But they haven't got a camera.	
– **Never mind.**	– Das macht nichts.

4 I, you, he, she, we, you, they:

Diese Wörter heißen persönliche Fürwörter, weil sie für andere Wörter in Sätzen stehen. Sie werden wie im Deutschen verwendet:

I	(ich)	**I**'m from Kaiserslautern.
you	(Du/Sie)	**You** must be Klaus.
he/she	(er/sie)	**He/She**'s from Liverpool.
we	(wir)	**We**'ve got a key.
you	(Ihr/Sie)	**You** must be Sam and Iris.
they	(sie)	**They** haven't got a dog.

1 What have you got?

camera video
telephone cat dog
German-English dictionary
television computer
photo of ...

Example: I've got a ... but I haven't got a ...

2 What have Mr and Mrs Wilson got?

✔	✘
television	video camera
cat	mountain bike
dictionary	dog
video	

1 They've got a television.
2 They haven't got a video camera.
3 ...

3 Please complete: have / haven't / got

– ..... you got an Eltro video?
– No, we ..... . But we've ..... a Sonics video.
– And ..... you got an Eltro video camera?
– Yes, we ..... .
– Oh, good.
– This is the camera and this is the Sonics video.

HOMESTUDY

Lerntip

Bereiten Sie sich auf die Homestudy-Seite vor, indem Sie zuerst die Teile des Step, die Sie im Kurs gemacht haben, noch einmal durchsehen. Dann probieren Sie die Übungen hier. Nehmen Sie dazu einen Bleistift. Überprüfen Sie Ihre Lösungen anhand des Schlüssels, unterstreichen Sie Fehler (falls es welche gibt!) und korrigieren Sie sie. Falls Ihnen nicht klar ist, warum Ihre Lösung nicht stimmt, fragen Sie Ihren Kursleiter / Ihre Kursleiterin. Alle Lösungen könnten Sie dann noch einmal ausradieren und die Übungen einige Tage später wiederholen, auch wenn sie vorher alle richtig waren. So sichern Sie Ihren Lernerfolg ab.

1 Crossword

Complete the crossword with:

T-I-N-A M-A-~~R~~-K V-~~A~~-~~N~~-E-S-~~S~~-~~A~~

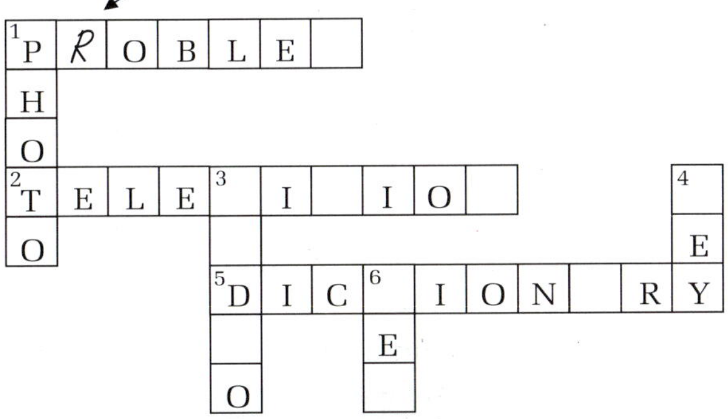

2 Please match.

1 Have you got a television?
2 Have you got a problem?
3 Have you got a video camera?
4 Have you got the key?
5 Have you got a photo of Paris?

☐ a No, I haven't. I'm OK.
☐ b Yes, I have, the key's here.
☐ c No, I haven't, but I've got a photo of London.
☐ d No I haven't, but I've got a camera.
☐ e Yes, I have. I've got a Sonics television.

3 Say it in English.

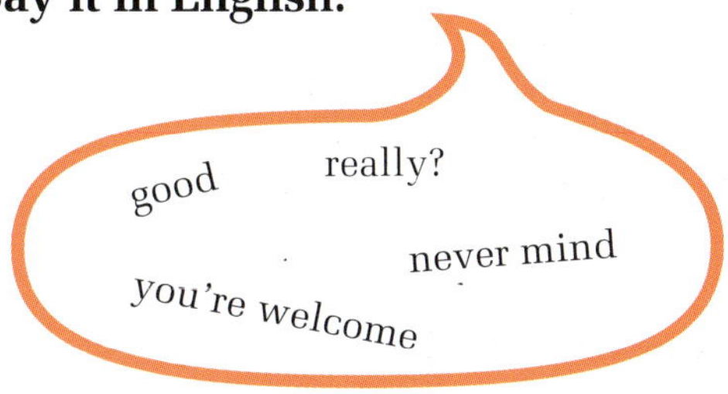

1 – They've got a photo of Michael Jackson.
– *Wirklich?* ...

2 – I haven't got a dictionary.
– *Es macht nichts.* ... I've got a German - English dictionary.

3 – Have you got the video camera?
– Yes, I have.
– *Prima* ...

4 – Thanks for the coffee.
– *Bitte.* ...

They've got a photo of London ...

STEP 2

Family and friends

STARTER

1 Revision

Make two teams and make sentences like this:

Team A: Video.
Team B: Have you got a video? *or:*
We've got a video. *or:*
We haven't got a video.
Team B: Problem
Team A: ...

problem cat you video 've we got haven't have? dog mountain bike dictionary

2 Vocabulary. Please complete.

Norman ⚭ Helen
John Vanessa

♂	♀
father	mother
husband	wife
son	daughter
brother	sister

1 Norman is Helen's husband.
Helen is Norman's ... .
2 John is Helen's son. Vanessa is Helen's ...
3 John is Vanessa's brother. Vanessa ...
4 Helen is Vanessa's mother. Norman ...

DIALOGUE

Part 1

Mark: This is a nice photo of your family.
Vanessa: Who's this?
Tina: It's my brother, Peter.
Vanessa: Are they his daughters?
Tina: Yes, and this is his wife, Susan.
Vanessa: Her hat's awful!

Part 2

Vanessa: Have Peter and Susan got a son?
Tina: Yes, he's a student.
Vanessa: Really? Where?
Tina: In San Francisco, Vanessa.
Vanessa: Oh.

ACTIVITIES

Part 1

1a Who's this?

Look at the pictures on page 18 and page 20 (Revision). Ask your partner questions like this:
Example:
A: Who's this? B: It's ...

1b Ask your partner.

Look at the picture in Part 1. A: you are a person in the photo. B: ask A questions; who is A?
Example:
B: Is this your wife? A: No, it isn't.
B: Is this your sister? A: Yes, it is.
B: Are you this person? A: Yes, I am.

1c What's his/her name?

Ask a partner. Example: Helen's husband.
A: What's his name? B: His name's Norman.

1 Helen's husband.
2 John's sister.
3 Tina's brother.
4 Peter's wife.
5 Norman's wife.
6 Vanessa's brother.
7 Susan's husband.
8 Peter's sister.

Part 2

2a Find someone who ...

Example: 2 brothers.
A: (Olaf), have you got two brothers?
B: No, I haven't.
A: (Hanni), have you got two brothers?
C: Yes, I have.

Ask questions and find students in your class with:

	Name of student(s)
2 brothers	
1 sister	
a friend in England	
2 daughters	
1 son	

2b Exchange information with your partner.

A: look at this page. B: look at page 112.

A: It is summer. Where are Mark and Tina's friends? Ask B questions and answer B's questions.
Example:
– Where is Barbara?
– She's in Freiburg.
– Where are Sven and Anita?
– They're in San Francisco.

Dennis	?
Barbara	Freiburg
Sven + Anita	San Francisco
Carmen + Glenn	?
Tom + Glenda	New York

2c And now you.

Talk to your partner about your family.
Example:
I've got 2 brothers. They are Hans and Klaus.
I've got a sister. Her name is ...
... is her husband.
My ... is ...

Listening & pronunciation

3a Listen again.

Listen to the dialogue parts 1-2 again.

3b Listen and complete: he's or his?

	1	2	3	4	5	6	7
he's	✓						
his							

3c Listen and answer.

Listen to the telephone conversation. What is the right answer? (→*Andere Länder, andere Sitten*)

1 What is the telephone number?
2 Where is John's wife?
3 Where are John's two sons?

GRAMMAR

1 Wie Sie Zugehörigkeit mit *'s* und *of* ausdrücken:

Helen**'s** husband Susan**'s** hat	**'s** wird bei Personen angefügt.
a photo **of** the house	**of** wird überwiegend bei Sachen vorangestellt.

2 Wie Sie Zugehörigkeit mit *my/your/...* ausdrücken:

Diese Wörter heißen besitzanzeigende Fürwörter. Und die gute Nachricht gleich vorweg: Die Verwendung dieser englischen Fürwörter ist wesentlich einfacher als im Deutschen, da sie grundsätzlich unveränderlich sind.

my	**my** father	mein (-e, -er, -es) usw.
your	**your** husband	dein/Ihr usw.
his	**his** daughter	sein usw.
her	**her** mother	ihr usw.
It's **my** brother, Peter.		Es ist mein Bruder Peter.
It's **my** sister, Susan.		Es ist meine Schwester Susan.

3 Aussagen mit *are* (das Verb *to be*):

We **are** / We'**re** ... You **are** / You'**re** ... They **are** / They'**re** ...	Wir sind ... Ihr seid ... Sie sind ...
They'**re** his daughters. They'**re** from Leipzig.	Sie sind seine Töchter. Sie kommen aus Leipzig.

Damit haben Sie alle Formen des Verbs *be*, des am häufigsten verwendeten englischen Verbs, kennengelernt.

4 Fragen mit Fragewort *who* und *where:*

Deutsch 'wer' ähnelt Englisch *where*. Und Englisch *who* erinnert an Deutsch'wo'. Doch Vorsicht, genau umgekehrt ist es: 'wer' = *who*; 'wo' = *where*.

Who's this? **Who** are they?	Wer ist das? Wer sind sie?
Where is she? **Where** are they?	Wo ist sie? Wo sind sie?

1 Lisa and you

I'm Lisa.
I'm from London.
My telephone number is 020 8627 5378.
I've got one son, his name is Roland, but I haven't got a daughter.
I've got a sister, her name's Sarah.

And now you. Write about your family.

2 Please complete: 's or s?

Peter and Susan have got two daughter... and one son. Peter... son, Simon, is in San Francisco. He... a student. Simon... sister... are eight and ten. They've got two cat... and one dog. The dog... name is Blackie.

3 They've got / They haven't got ...

Mr & Mrs Brent	Mr & Mrs Wilson
telephone x2 daughter x2 camera x3 television x2 video x1	telephone x1 son x3 dictionary x1 television x1 cat x3

Make sentences like this:
The Wilsons have got a telephone.
The Brents have got two daughters.
They haven't got a ...

4 Please complete: Who, how or where?

1 A: ..... are your two sons?
B: They're in America.
2 A: ..... is on the phone?
B: It's John.
3 A: ..... is your husband?
B: He's fine, thanks.
4 A: ..... is this in the photo?
B: It's my sister.

HOMESTUDY

Lerntip

Wenn Sie ein neues Wort hören, das Sie lernen möchten, werden Sie es wahrscheinlich aufschreiben wollen. Das können Sie z.B. in ein Vokabelheft oder auf Karteikarten. Karteikarten haben mehrere Vorteile: Sie können sie unterschiedlich ordnen, z.B. alphabetisch, nach Themen oder nach Wichtigkeit. Es ist ausreichend Platz, um später etwas nachzutragen. Außerdem können Sie jederzeit ein paar in der Tasche mitnehmen, wenn Sie unterwegs lernen wollen. Welche Methode Sie auch wählen, eines ist wichtig: Notieren Sie nie nur ein Einzelwort mit Übersetzung, sondern immer einen Satzzusammenhang. Anstatt: Welcome = Willkommen, notieren Sie z.B.: Welcome to King's Lynn = Willkommen in King's Lynn. So lernen Sie gleichzeitig die Bedeutung und wie das Wort benutzt wird.

1 Please complete: my/your/his/her.

M: Vanessa, is this ..... mother in the hat?
V: Yes, it's my mother in ..... awful hat,
and this is ..... brother, John.
M: And who's this?
V: It's Henry Wilson. He's nice.
..... wife isn't in the photo.

2 Find eight words.

F	A	T	H	E	R	T	U	R	A	F
T	A	B	W	G	C	A	V	M	B	N
M	H	A	W	I	F	E	K	B	L	H
O	O	E	R	O	T	H	O	R	C	U
T	T	B	L	E	T	S	R	O	N	S
H	H	T	S	S	O	N	U	T	S	B
E	L	L	P	U	A	N	T	H	O	A
R	O	S	I	S	T	E	R	E	E	N
S	A	D	D	B	I	C	H	R	D	D
N	N	E	D	A	U	G	H	T	E	R

3 Please complete.

Stanley ∞ Maria

James ∞ Barbara   Michael ∞ Caroline

Andrew   Samantha

My name is Michael. My father's name is Stanley and my mother's name ..... Maria. They'..... nice. I've ..... a brother but I haven't got a sister. James is ..... brother. Barbara is ..... wife. They've got one ..... . He's a student in London. Caroline is my ..... . We've ..... one daughter. ..... name is Samantha.

4 Say it in English. Please match.

1 Sie möchten wissen, wer jemand auf einem Foto ist.
2 Man sagt Ihnen: 'Das ist mein Bruder'.
3 Sie fragen, wo er sich aufhält.
4 Sie wollen wissen, wie es ihm geht.
5 Man sagt Ihnen: 'Es geht ihm sehr gut'.

☐ a How is he?
☐ b He's fine, thanks.
☐ c It's my brother.
☐ d Where is he?
☐ e Who is this?

Susan's son is a student in San Francisco.

STEP 3

Shops and places

STARTER

1 Revision

Ihre Kursleiterin / Ihr Kursleiter zeichnet ihren/ seinen Stammbaum an die Tafel. Beschreiben Sie die Familie. Example:
You've got one brother. His name's Sam. You...

2 Vocabulary

Look at this list of words: museum, shop, restaurant, pub, disco. Match three of them with the pictures here.

1

2

3

DIALOGUE

Part 1

Tina: Where's my hairdryer, Mark, have you got it?
Mark: No, it must be in Hamburg, too.
Tina: Oh, no.
Vanessa: Never mind, ask my mother, she's got two hairdryers.
Tina: Oh good.

Part 2

Mark: What's King's Lynn like, Vanessa?
Vanessa: Oh, it's got nice shops.
Mark: Has it got a good restaurant?
Vanessa: Yes, but Cambridge has got a lot of nice restaurants and it's a very interesting place.
Mark: Really?

Part 3

Mark: Has King's Lynn got a museum?
Vanessa: Yes, it's got two. And it's got three discos and um, six jeans shops ...
Tina: And it's got fifteen pubs. Wenns is a nice pub, Mark, and it's very near here. Let's have a drink.
Mark: OK. Good idea. Let's go to Wenns.
Mark and Tina: Goodbye, Vanessa.

ACTIVITIES

Part 1

1a What has he/she got?

1 Helen has got two hairdryers.
2 Norman … a son John.
3 Tina …
4 Vanessa …
5 My partner …

1b Ask your teacher.

Ihre Kursleiterin / Ihr Kursleiter zeichnet ein Strichmännchen an die Tafel.

Teacher: This is my father/ sister/friend/...

Ask your teacher questions. What has the father/ sister/friend/... got?
Example:
Has he/she got a computer? – No, he/she hasn't.
Has he/she got a sister? – Yes, he/she has.

Now ask your partner.
A: This is my ... B: Has he/she got ...?

Part 2

2a Ask your partner.

Example:
A: What's (Germany) like?
B: It's (interesting).

awful not very nice OK
nice / interesting / good
very nice / very interesting / very good

1 Germany/Austria/ Switzerland
2 Television here in ...
3 … (= *sein / ihr Wohnort*)
4 England
5 English tea
6 English Network

2b Ask your teacher about a place.

What's ... like?
Is it a(n) nice / interesting / good / awful /… place?
Has it got shops / a museum /…?
Is it / Are they …?

Now ask your partner about a place.

Part 3

3a Numbers 11-20

Say: 1, 2, 3, 4, 5, 6, 7, 8, 9, 10.

Now listen and repeat these numbers:

11 eleven	15 fifteen	19 nineteen
12 twelve	16 sixteen	20 twenty
13 thirteen	17 seventeen	
14 fourteen	18 eighteen	

3b Bingo

Tragen Sie 6 Zahlen zwischen 1 und 20 hier ein. Ein Kursmitglied ruft Zahlen in willkürlicher Reihenfolge aus, z.B. *Two, nineteen, eleven, ...* Streichen Sie die genannten Zahlen bei sich durch. Wer zuerst alle 6 Zahlen durchgestrichen hat, ruft *Bingo!*

Listening & pronunciation

4a Listen again.

Listen to the dialogue parts 1-3 again.

4b Listen and repeat: [ə]

Achten Sie auf die Buchstaben, die **fett** gedruckt sind. Sie sind alle derselbe Laut.

a comput**er**
seven camer**a**s
the fath**er**
a lot **of** stud**e**nts
a lot **of** ban**a**n**a**s

nice t**o** meet you
where **are** you from
have **a** seat
cup **of** tea
tea **a**nd biscuits

4c Listen and answer.

John and Chris are in King's Lynn. Listen and answer the question. What is right? Chris:

GRAMMAR

1 Wie Sie Auskünfte über einen Ort erfragen können:

What's ... like?	Wie ist ...? Was ist in ... los?

2 Wie Sie jemanden auffordern, etwas mit Ihnen zu unternehmen:

– **Let's** go to the pub.	Laß/Laßt uns in die Kneipe gehen.
– Yes, good idea. **Let's** have a drink.	Laß/Laßt uns mal was trinken.

3 Das Hauptwort:

Haupt- oder Namenwörter werden benutzt, um Menschen, Tieren, Dingen und abstrakten Begriffen ihren Namen zu geben.
In der Regel werden die englischen Hauptwörter (*family, photo*) klein geschrieben; Eigennamen aber werden wie im Deutschen groß geschrieben (*Peter, King's Lynn*).
Die Mehrzahl von Hauptwörtern wird im Englischen im Normalfall durch Anfügung eines *-s* gebildet. Dieses *s* wird unterschiedlich ausgesprochen, je nachdem welcher Laut ihm vorausgeht. Sie werden die unterschiedlichen Aussprachen automatisch richtig bilden, wenn Sie flüssig sprechen.

Aussprache [s] wie ein deutsches ß	Aussprache [z] wie deutsch 'sausen'	Aussprache [ɪz] nach Zischlauten
shop**s** drink**s**	pub**s** museum**s**	place**s**

4 *Has got* in Aussage- und Fragesätzen:

He/She has got (= He's/She's got) two computers.
Has Cambridge got a good restaurant?
Yes, **it has got (= it's got)** a lot of nice restaurants.

Die Form *has got / 's got* gilt für *he/she/it* und für Hauptwörter, die durch *he/she/it* ersetzt werden könnten (z.B. Peter, Mary, the photo). In allen anderen Fällen heißt es *have got / 've got.*

1 Please complete: has got / hasn't got.

1 Tina .... her hairdryer in King's Lynn; it's in Hamburg. But Vanessa's mother .... two hairdryers.
2 Mark .... his video camera in King's Lynn; it's in Hamburg, too.
3 King's Lynn .... a good restaurant but Cambridge .... a lot of nice restaurants.
4 Cambridge .... a lot of discos and nice pubs, too.
5 The museum .... a lot of very interesting photos of Cambridge.

2 Please complete.

got has an
has what´s got

(M = Mark, V = Vanessa)
V: (1) Hamburg like, Mark? (2) it got good discos?
M: Yes, it (3)
V: And has it (4) good pubs?
M: Yes, and it's got (5) English pub, too.
V: Really?
M: And it's (6) a good museum.
V: Oh, museums are awful.

3 And now you.

Write about your place or city.

museum hotel
disco good park
shop interesting pub
restaurant bank
nice awful a lot of

Example:
... has got ... and it's got ...
but it hasn't got ...

HOMESTUDY

Lerntip

Manche Leute machen sich das Leben und vor allem das Sprachenlernen unnötig schwer, weil sie die Vorstellung haben, sie wollen Englisch oder irgendeine Sprache "perfekt" beherrschen, und wenn das nicht geht, geben sie bald entnervt auf. Es klingt vielleicht komisch, aber wenn wir uns wirklich brauchbare Sprachfertigkeiten aneignen wollen, müssen wir uns den Perfektionismus abschminken. Das heißt nicht, daß wir schlampig oder nachlässig sein wollen, vielmehr sollten wir uns realistische, "kleine" Ziele setzen und diese Schritt für Schritt verfolgen. Dann erreichen wir sie auch!

1 Who is it: Vanessa/Tina/Norman/ Karen?

1 She's got a brother and his name's John. Her name's ...
2 He's from Wales and he and his wife have got a bed and breakfast. His name's ...
3 She's from King's Lynn and she's got a sister in Germany. Her ...
4 She's from England but now she's from Hamburg in Germany. ...

2 Odd man out.

Welches Wort gehört nicht zu den anderen drei?

1 awful	(hairdryer)	nice	interesting
2 thanks	thirteen	five	nineteen
3 camera	television	video	key
4 husband	student	wife	daughter
5 museum	restaurant	pub	dictionary
6 his	her	my	who
7 Austria	Germany	Wales	London

3 What has Mrs Penny got?

television	2
computer	–
hotel	–
hat	4
friend	5

1 She's got 2 televisions.
2 She hasn't ... computer.
3 ...
4 ...
5 ...

4 Say it in English. Please match.

Sie wollen wissen, ob
1 die Stadt ein interessantes Museum hat.
2 die Kneipe in der Nähe vom Museum ist.
3 die Kneipe nett ist.
4 die Stadt ein gutes Restaurant hat.
5 die Stadt viele nette Geschäfte hat.

☐ a Has it got a good restaurant?
☐ b Has it got a lot of nice shops?
☐ c Is the pub nice?
☐ d Has it got an interesting museum?
☐ e Is the pub near the museum?

Shops in King's Lynn High Street

REVISION AND EXTENSION

• Starter

Look at the picture.
What has Mr Denton got?
He's got a swimming pool.
He's got a ...

1 Please complete: have got or haven't got?

Sam and Sandy ..... got jeans and a lot of T-shirts but they ..... got a pullover. They ..... got a camera and they ..... got a film. They ..... two books but they ..... a dictionary. Sam and Sandy ..... a hairdryer.

2 Four questions.

Make four questions and ask a partner.

1 Where ...? 3 Who ...?
2 What ...? 4 How ...?

3 Your class list

Ask 3 students in the class: Have you got a ..... ?

Name	Cat	Dog	Camera	Television	Computer
Christian	✗	✓2	✓	✓	✗

✓= yes ✗= no

OK? Now tell the class.

Example:
Christian hasn't got a cat but he has got two dogs.
He has got a camera and a television but he hasn't got a computer.
(Silvia) ...
(Hans) ...

4 A number game

Machen Sie einen Papierball. Fangen Sie bei 20 an und zählen Sie rückwärts. Derjenige, dem der Ball zugeworfen wird, muß schnell die nächstniedrigere Zahl sagen: 20 - 19 - ...

5 Let's have a drink.

Machen Sie Vorschläge, wo Sie nach dem Kurs mit Ihrer Klasse hingehen wollen.

Let's go to ...
Good idea!
Oh, no, let's go to ...
O.K.
Let's have a ...
Super!
Oh, no, not ...
It's awful!
Yes, good idea. Let's go to ...

REVISION AND EXTENSION

6 Please complete.

daughter husband father son
brother sister mother
She's He's

Queen Elizabeth:
1 "This is Prince Philip. He's my husband."
2 "This is Prince Andrew. ..... my ..... ."
3 "This is Princess Anne. ..... my ..... ."

Prince Andrew:
4 "This is Queen Elizabeth. ..... my ..... ."
5 "This is Prince Charles. ..... my ..... ."
6 "This is Princess Anne. ..... my ..... ."
7 "This is Prince Philip. ..... my ..... ."

7 And you?

Have you got a picture of your family? What can you say?
This is my ... This is ...

8 Memory check

Welche Wörter fallen Ihnen spontan ein, die Sie in Unit 2 gelernt haben? Schreiben Sie sie auf und vergleichen Sie Ihre Liste mit der Ihres Nachbarn / Ihrer Nachbarin.

9 Reading

Helen Kemp is from King's Lynn. Helen's got one son. His name is John. And she's got one daughter. Her name is Vanessa. Helen's husband's name is Norman. Helen has got two brothers. Her brother James and his wife Peggy are in Australia. They have got three daughters but they haven't got a son. Her brother Alan and his girlfriend Susan are in Scotland.
Helen has got a hobby – it is writing postcards.

Option:
Schreiben Sie zu Hause Ihrem Kursleiter / Ihrer Kursleiterin einen Brief über sich selbst und Ihre Familie. Beginnen Sie so:
Dear ...,
My name is ...
I am from ...
I have got ...
He's/She's/They've got/ They're ...

• Useful phrases

Extra 1

Song

Number 7

Listen and complete.

7 ... 6 ... 5 ... 4 ... 3 ... 2 ... 1 ...
take off!

..... is my favourite number
..... is the number for me
He's on flight ....
On a Boeing ....
And he's only ..... hours away
from me
Only ..... hours away from me.

Good morning, hallo darling,
Is that .... ?
Good morning, hallo darling,
Yes it's me, I'm on the line.
Good morning, hallo darling,
The sky above is blue.
Good morning, hallo darling,
Goodbye and I love you.

Crossword

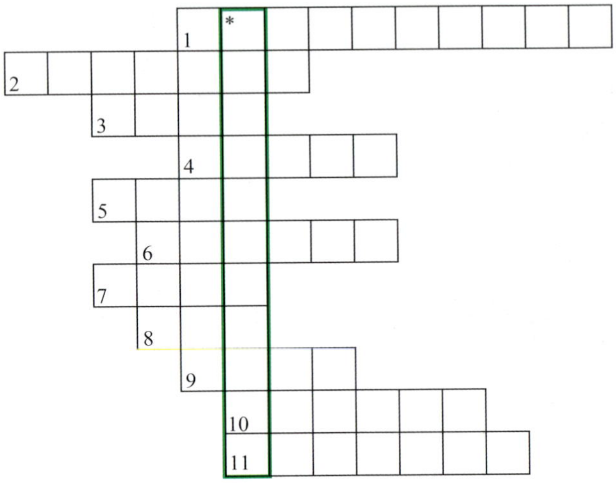

1 Have you got an English-English ..... ?
2 This is my son, my daughter and my ..... .
3 Nice to ..... you.
4 I haven't got my camera. - Oh, ... mind.
5 The bank is ..... the museum.
6 Vanessa, an ice-cream? - Yes, ...
7 .....'..... go to the pub and have a drink.
8 I've got a brother ..... I haven't got a sister.
9 How are you? - ....., thanks.
10 What's your phone ..... ?
11 I'm from Hamburg in ..... .

* The mystery word: English is ..... .

Odd man out

1 brother wife mother student	2 dictionary radio stereo set computer	3 restaurant drink pub disco	4 apple coffee orange banana	5 fine awful interesting nice

Extra 1

Spotlight

A famous number

'Number 10' is number 10 Downing Street, in London. It's the home of the British Prime Minister. It is near Buckingham Palace, the home of the Queen.

10 Downing Street is often on television, with two English 'bobbies' or policemen. But number 11 is not so famous. Number 11 is the home of one of the ministers.

The matchstick game

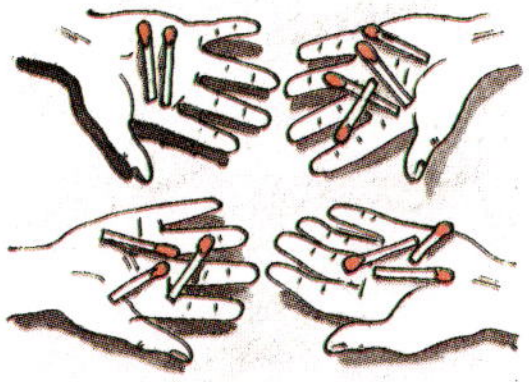

Bilden Sie Gruppen zu viert. Jede(r) versteckt 1, 2, 3, 4 oder 5 Streichhölzer in der Hand. Dann legen alle die geschlossene Hand auf den Tisch und raten, wieviele Streichhölzer insgesamt auf dem Tisch sind. Wenn alle geraten haben, legen Sie die Hölzer auf den Tisch und zählen Sie sie. Wer die Zahl geraten hat oder ihr am nächsten kommt, hat gewonnen.

How many have we got?
Ah! ...
Let's see.
We've got ...
You win.

Chain game

A: My brother has got a cat.
B: My brother has got a cat and he has got a camera.
C: My brother has got a cat and he has got a camera and he has got a ...
D: ...
E: ...

Getting about

Unit 3

Mark und Tina erkunden die nahe Umgebung, gehen einkaufen und treffen sich mit John und Chris im Pub. In dieser Unit lernen Sie u.a.:

- nach dem Weg fragen und Wegbeschreibungen geben
- einkaufen und nach Preisen fragen
- sagen und fragen, was man mag
- die Uhrzeit.

STEP 1

At the shop

STARTER

Numbers 21-100

Listen and repeat.

21 twenty-one	34 thirty-four	56 fifty-six	80 eighty
22 twenty-two	40 forty	60 sixty	90 ninety
23 twenty-three	45 forty-five	67 sixty-seven	100 a hundred
30 thirty	50 fifty	70 seventy	one hundred

Now write 9 numbers from 1-100. Say the numbers to your partner. He/She writes the numbers down.

DIALOGUE

Part 1

Helen: Hello, Mark. How are you?
Mark: Hello, I'm fine.
Helen: Is the house OK?
Mark: Yes, we're very happy. Oh, Helen, where's the nearest shop?
Helen: Here in Bridge Street. Go along Bridge Street and it's on the left.

Part 2

Mark: Have you got a map of King's Lynn?
Shopkeeper: Yes, here.
Mark: How much is it?
Shopkeeper: It's £3.10.
Mark: And how much are the postcards?
Shopkeeper: They're 20p.

Part 3

Mark: And 5 stamps, please.
Shopkeeper: Sorry, we haven't got stamps. But the post office is here in Bridge Street.
Mark: Oh, yes, where is it?
Shopkeeper: Turn right and it's opposite the pub ... next to the video shop. Um ... five postcards and a map, is that all?
Mark: Yes, that's all.
Shopkeeper: £4.10, please.
(→ *Andere Länder, andere Sitten*)

ACTIVITIES

Part 1

1a It's on the left/right.

Ask and answer questions. You are at (x).
A: Where's the nearest ...?
B: Go along Bridge Street and it's on the left/ right.

1 pub	3 disco	5 museum
2 restaurant	4 video shop	6 bank

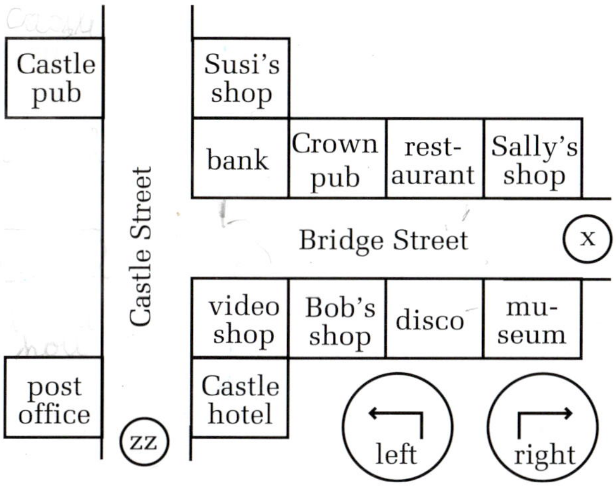

Part 2

2a Ask and answer with your partner.

1 How much ..... the postcards? – They're 20p.
2 How much ..... the map? – It's £1.20.
3 How much ..... the biscuits? – They're 49p.
4 How much ..... the dictionary? – It's £5.99.
5 How much ..... the camera? – It's £59.95.
6 How much ..... the bananas? – They're 73p.

2b Exchange information with your partner.

A: look at this page. B: look at page 112.
A: You work in a shop in London.
B is a tourist. Answer B's questions.

Map £2.50	Hat £13.29
Postcards 15p	Cup £5.99
Camera £26.95	Biscuits £3.95
Dictionary £8.99	

Part 3

3a Where's ...?

Look at the map in 1a.
The bank is **next to** the pub.
The bank is **opposite** the video shop.
1 Where is the restaurant? – It's...
2 Where is the disco? ...
3 Where is the post office? ...
4 Where is Sally's shop? ...

3b Memory game

Look at Bridge Street and Castle Street in 1a for one minute, then close your book. You are at (zz). Ask your partner questions.

Example: A: Where is the ...?
B: Go along Castle Street.
(Turn ...)
The ... is on the ...
It's next to/opposite ...

Listening & pronunciation

4a Listen again.

Listen to the dialogue parts 1-3 again.

4b Listen and repeat:[θ]

Der Laut *th* klingt für deutsche Ohren ungewöhnlich, ist aber nicht so schwer, wenn Sie dabei herzhaft lispeln!

1 **th**ree – seven
2 **th**irteen – seventeen
3 **th**irty – seventy
4 **th**irty-**th**ree – seventy-seven
5 **th**irty-seven – seventy-**th**ree

4c Listen and match.

Look at the map in 1a. You are at (zz). Match the dialogues on the cassette and the places.

Dialogue 1 ☐ a The disco.
Dialogue 2 ☐ b The restaurant.
Dialogue 3 ☐ c The Castle pub.

GRAMMAR

1 Wie Sie nach Preisen fragen:

Sie setzen den Ausdruck *How much* mit *is* oder *are* ein, um zu erfahren, wieviel etwas kostet:

How much *is* a map of Chester? – It's £3.10.
are the postcards? – They're 20p.

2 Wie Sie nach dem Weg fragen:

Where is the nearest bank?
's the nearest post office?

3 Wie Sie Wegbeschreibungen geben:

Go along River Street.	Gehen Sie / Geh die River Street weiter.
Turn right/left ...	Biegen Sie / Bieg rechts/ links ein ...

Benutzen Sie stets nur die Grundform der Verben, wenn Sie eine oder mehrere Personen wie oben auffordern wollen, etwas zu tun:

Come in.	Komm / Kommen Sie herein.
Have a seat.	Nimm / Nehmen Sie Platz.

4 Wie Sie Ortsangaben machen:

Den Standort einer Person bzw. die Lage von einem Gebäude, Zimmer oder Geschäft können Sie so beschreiben:

Near — next to — opposite — on the left — on the right

5 Der bestimmte Artikel *the*:

In Unit 1 haben Sie den unbestimmten Artikel *a/an* kennengelernt. Der bestimmte Artikel lautet in der Ein- und Mehrzahl durchweg *the*. Er wird aber vor Mitlauten (b, p, t, m usw.) und Selbstlauten (a, e, i, o, u) verschieden ausgesprochen.

Aussprache: [ðə]	Aussprache: [ðɪ]
the postcard	**the** American
the maps	**the** Americans

1 Match the number and the word.

25 ☐ a thirty-one
14 ☐ b fifty-six
56 ☐ c twenty-five
97 ☐ d eighty-three
83 ☐ e fourteen
72 ☐ f ninety-seven
31 ☐ g forty-eight
48 ☐ h seventy-two

2 Ask and answer questions.

– How much is/are ...
– It's/They're ...

map of London	£2.60
stamps	£0.78
dictionary	£12.75
television	£99.99
hat	£7.75
postcards	£1.20
T shirt	£6.39
dog	£50.75

1 How much is the map of London? – It's two pounds sixty.

3 Please complete the dialogue.

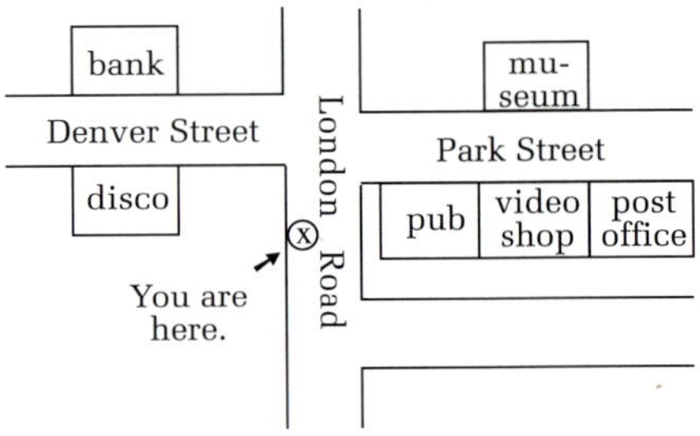

A: Excuse me, where's the nearest post office.
B: Go ...
A: And where's the nearest bank?
B: Turn ...
A: Thank you very much. Goodbye.

HOMESTUDY

Lerntip

Natürlich wollen Sie nicht nur sprechen lernen; Sie wollen auch verstehen, was man Ihnen auf Englisch sagt. Aber auch das Hörverständnis kommt nicht von selbst, es muß eingeübt werden. Verstehen lernt man durch bewußtes, systematisches, wiederholtes Zuhören. Hören Sie den englischen Stimmen auf der Cassette gut zu, und zwar möglichst ohne den gedruckten Text gleichzeitig mitzulesen. Hören Sie die Texte immer mehrere Male. Entspannen Sie sich beim Zuhören und lassen Sie sich nicht durch unbekannte Wörter oder unbekannte Grammatik aus der Fassung bringen. Beim ersten Zuhören werden Sie manches nicht verstehen, bei jeder Wiederholung verstehen Sie jedoch etwas mehr.

1 Match the questions and the answers.

1 How much are the postcards?
2 How much is the map of Bristol?
3 Is that all?
4 Have you got stamps?

☐ a It's £3.10
☐ b Yes. That's all, thank you.
☐ c Sorry, no, we haven't.
☐ d They're 20p.

3 Ask questions with: who/where/how/what/how much?

1 ... – They're Henry and Mary Wilson.
2 ... – He's in London.
3 ... – She's fine.
4 ... – He's got a map.
5 ... – The map is £4.50.

4 Please complete.

Look at number 3 on page 48 and complete the dialogue.

on | next to | opposite | in

A: Where's the video shop?
B: It's ..... the post office, ... the museum.
A: Is it ..... London Road?
B: No, it's ..... Park Street. Turn right and it's ..... the right.
A: Thank you very much.

5 Say it in English. Please match and complete.

Sie wollen wissen:
1 was die Postkarte kostet.
2 was die Briefmarken kosten.
3 wo die nächste Post ist.
4 ob das Geschäft einen Stadtplan von King's Lynn hat.

☐ a ... the stamps?
☐ b ... map of King's Lynn?
☐ c ... the postcard?
☐ d ... post office, please?

STEP 2

At the pub

STARTER

1 Revision

Ein Kursmitglied nennt eine Zahl zwischen 11 und 100 und wirft einen (Papier-)Ball einem zweiten Kursmitglied zu. Dieses nennt eine andere Zahl, die mit der letzten Ziffer seiner Zahl beginnt, usw. Zum Beispiel:

2③ → 3⑤ → 5② → 2⑨ → 9⑤

2 Vocabulary

Food	Drink
hamburger	tea
steak	coffee
…	…

What other English words do you know?

DIALOGUE

Part 1

John: ... and the English beer for you, Mark. Cheers!
All: Cheers!
Chris: Is it OK, Mark? Do you like it?
Mark: Yes, I do. It's ... er ... interesting.
Tina: Do you drink English beer, Chris?
Chris: No, I don't. I don't like it very much.
Tina: Do you like English food?
Chris: Yes, I do.

Part 2

Chris: I eat English food, fish and chips and ... but I like my hamburgers and my coke, too!
Mark: Do you work for McBurger's, Chris?
Chris: No, I don't. I work for Procomp, an American computer firm. And you?
Mark: Oh, I work for the Bundesbahn, the German State Railways.
Chris: Really?

Part 3

Tina: What time is it?
John: It's three o' clock.
Mark: Do pubs close in the afternoon in England?
Tina: Yes, a lot of pubs do. Let's go.
(→ *Andere Länder, andere Sitten*)

ACTIVITIES

Part 1

1a Ask your teacher.

Example:
You: Do you like tea/ice-cream/German television/...?
T: Yes, I do. / No, I don't.
Here are ten ideas: Beethoven? London? beer? pubs? discos? English food? coffee? English tea? bananas? your city/place?
Now ask your partner.

Part 2

2a Find two students who ...

What do you like? Write 8 things.

I eat:	I drink:
1 *pizza*	5 ...
2 ...	6 ...
3 ...	7 ...
4 ...	8 ...

Now find two students with the same thing. Ask questions like this:

Do you eat (pizza), (Olaf)? – No, I don't.
Do you eat (pizza), (Hanni)? – Yes, I do. (*Write Hanni's name.*)
Do you eat (pizza), (Heinz)? – Yes, I do. (*Write Heinz's name.*)

I eat:	Names:
1 *pizza*	*Hanni, Heinz*

Ok? Now tell the class.

Example:
I eat (pizza). (Hanni) und (Heinz) eat pizza, too.

2b Do you work for ...?

Schreiben Sie auf einen Zettel (ohne Ihren Namen), wo Sie arbeiten, z. B.:
I work for (Vitex) in (Essen). *or:*
I work for the state. *or:*
I work for a (bank). *or:*
I work at home.

Ihr Kursleiter / Ihre Kursleiterin sammelt alle Zettel ein. Von ihm/ihr erhalten Sie einen anderen Zettel zurück. Wessen Zettel? Stellen Sie anderen Kursmitgliedern Fragen, bis Sie das richtige Kursmitglied gefunden haben:
Do you work for ... (in ...)? – Yes, I do. / No, I don't.

Part 3

3a What time is it?

Listen and repeat the times:

1.00 one o'clock
2.05 two oh five
3.15 three fifteen
4.30 four thirty
5.45 five forty-five
6.50 six fifty
7.55 seven fifty-five

Now tell your teacher. What time is it?

Now write down five times. Then tell your partner. He/She writes down the times, too.

Listening & pronunciation

4a Listen again.

Listen to the dialogue parts 1-3 again.

4b Listen and repeat: [e] –[æ]

yes – thanks
ten – hat
pen – map
left – stamp
welcome – hamburger
very – apple
seven – sandwich

4c Listen and answer.

Listen to the interviews. What do they say?

1 ☐ a I work for an English firm.
☐ b I work for an American firm.
2 ☐ a I work for the German State Railways.
☐ b I work for the German Post Office.
3 ☐ a I work at home.
☐ b I work in a hotel.

GRAMMAR

1 Wie Sie Aussagesätze in der Gegenwart bilden:

Im Englischen werden Aussagesätze wie im Deutschen gebildet.

I eat a lot of English food.	Ich esse viele englische Speisen.
You work for the Bundesbahn.	Sie arbeiten / Du arbeitest für die Bundesbahn.
We drink coffee.	Wir trinken Kaffee.
Pubs/They close in the afternoon.	Kneipen / Sie schließen nachmittags.

2 Wie Sie Fragen mit *do* bilden:

Fragen, die mit *is/are/has/have* eingeleitet werden, kennen Sie schon. Die meisten anderen Fragen in der Gegenwart werden mit *do* eingeleitet. Sie können *do* also als Signal für Fragen in der Gegenwart ansehen.

⚠

Do you eat a lot of English food?
Do you work for the Bundesbahn?
Do pubs/they close in the afternoon?

3 Kurzantworten in der Gegenwart mit *do:*

Antworten auf Fragen wie in Abschnitt 2 können 'Ja' oder 'Nein' lauten. Nehmen Sie das erstgenannte Verb der Frage, also *do*, in Ihrer Antwort nach *Yes* oder *No* wieder auf.

Fragen	Kurzantworten
Do you like television?	Yes, I **do.** No, I **don't.**
Do museums close ...?	Yes, they **do.** No, they **don't.**

1 Answer the questions.

Example: Do you like ...?
– Yes, I do. It's/They're very nice.
– No, I don't. It's/They're not very nice.

1 Do you like coke?
2 Do you like television?
3 Do you like hamburgers?
4 Do you like discos?
5 Do you like whisky?
6 Do you like bananas?

2 Make questions. Then answer them.

Do they:

like drink eat work go	for a bank? to discos? bananas? coffee? television?

3 Please match.

1 1.30	☐	a two o'clock
2 2.45	☐	b eight fifty-five
3 7.15	☐	c eleven ten
4 12.05	☐	d two forty-five
5 11.10	☐	e seven fifteen
6 9.20	☐	f nine twenty
7 8.55	☐	g twelve oh five
8 2.00	☐	h one thirty

HOMESTUDY

Lerntip

Sie werden sicher längst gemerkt haben, daß das Sprachenlernen nicht von heute auf morgen geht und auch nicht von alleine, sondern nur durch fortgesetztes, regelmäßiges Üben, sowohl im Unterricht als auch zu Hause. Nehmen Sie Ihr Lernen selbst in die Hand, indem Sie selbst entscheiden, welche von den vielen Wörtern und Redewendungen für Sie am wichtigsten sind.

1 Please complete the dialogue.

0.00 – 12.00 is *in the morning*
12.00 – 18.00 is *in the afternoon*
18.00 – 23.00 is *in the evening*

am = 0.00 – 12.00
pm = 12.00 – 24.00

Closing	Times
Museums	4.30 pm
Post offices	5.30 pm
Banks	4.30 pm
Shops	5.30 pm
Restaurants	11.30 pm
Discos	2.00 am

A: What time do the museums close in King's Lynn?
B: At four-thirty in the ..... .
A: And when ..... the post offices close?
B: They close at five thirty ..... the afternoon.
A: ..... the banks close at 5 o'clock?
B: No, they ..... . They close at four thirty.
A: Has King's Lynn got a disco?
B: Yes, It ..... . It's got three. The discos ..... at two o'clock in the morning.
(→ *Andere Länder, andere Sitten*)

2 Make questions and answer them: Yes, they do. / No, they don't.

pub ✘
coke ✘
McBurger's ✔
computer firm ✘
bank ✔
disco ✔
fish and chips ✔

Example:
– Do they work for a computer firm?
– No, they don't.

1 they/work for/computer firm/?
2 they/work for/bank/?
3 they/like/English food/?
4 they/drink/coke/?
5 they/go to/discos/?
6 they/go to/pubs/?
7 they/eat/hamburgers/?

3 Say it in English. Please match.

Was sagt man, wenn man:
1 die Uhrzeit wissen will?
2 wissen will, ob jemand etwas mag?
3 etwas nicht besonders mag?
4 beim Trinken anstößt?
5 wissen will, ob jemand Tee trinkt?

☐ a Do you drink tea?
☐ b What time is it?
☐ c Cheers!
☐ d I don't like it very much.
☐ e Do you like it?

The opening times of a King's Lynn bank

STEP 3

A game of tennis

STARTER

1 Revision

Look at the closing times on page 53 again, for one minute. Then listen to your teacher's questions and answer. Example:

Teacher: Do the banks close at 11.00 in the morning?
You: No, they don't.
Teacher: Do ...
You: Yes, they do. / No, they don't.

2 Vocabulary

What sports and games do you know in English? A lot of words are international.

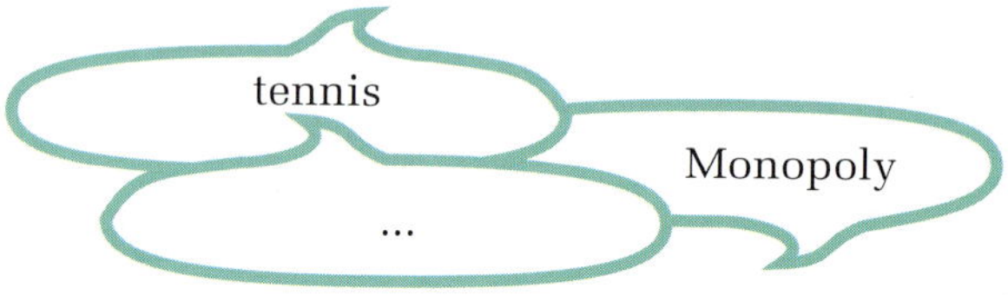

DIALOGUE

Part 1

Chris: Do you play tennis, Tina?
Tina: Yes, I do. I like tennis. Why do you ask?
Chris: Oh, I play a lot of tennis!
Tina: Where do you play?
Chris: Here in King's Lynn, at the new sports centre.

Part 2

Chris: And you, Mark? Do you play tennis?
Mark: No, I don't. I don't like tennis. It's not very exciting.
Chris: So you haven't got a partner here in King's Lynn, Tina?
Tina: No, I haven't.

Part 3

Tina: When do you usually play, Chris? At the weekend?
Chris: Yes, I play on Saturday. Have you got time on Saturday?
Tina: Yes, I have.
Chris: Well, let's have a game.
Tina: Good idea.
Chris: Is 11 o'clock OK?
Tina: Yes, that's great.
Chris: Good!

ACTIVITIES

Part 1

1a Do you play ...? Where do you play ...?

What games/sports do you like? Write down 5. Ask your teacher for help ('What's ... in English ?').
Now ask your partner. Example:
A: Do you play tennis?
B: No, I don't.
A: Do you play Monopoly?
B: Yes, I do.
A: Where do you play Monopoly?
B: I play at home.

Part 2

2a Talk about Helen and Norman.

beer ✗ tennis ✓ television ✗
squash ✗ apples ✓
bananas ✗ computer ✓ coffee ✓
Elvis Presley ✓ Wagner ✗

What do/don't they like/play/eat/drink? Make sentences:
1 They play tennis.
2 They don't play squash.
...

2b And now you.

What do/don't you like?
Say four positive and four negative sentences with: like, eat, drink, play.

Part 3

3a The days of the week

Listen and repeat:

Monday
Tuesday
Wednesday
Thursday
Friday
Saturday
Sunday

Saturday and Sunday are the weekend.

3b At or on?

at the weekend	on Wednesday

Tuesday	Saturday	3 o'clock
the weekend	10 o'clock	Wednesday
11.30	Monday	Sunday

3c Ask your partner.

A: Do you (play) (squash)?
B: Yes, I do. / No, I don't.
A: When do you usually (play)?
B: I usually (play) (on Saturday at 8 o'clock).

Here are eight ideas.

play	drink	go
tennis squash	tea coffee beer	to the pub to the English class to work

Listening & pronunciation

4a Listen again.

Listen to the dialogue parts 1-3 again.

4b Listen and repeat.

1 When do you play tennis?
2 Where do you play tennis?
3 What's English food like?
4 What time is it?
5 Where are you from?
6 Why do you ask?
7 What's the problem?

4c Listen and answer.

Listen to John Biggs. He is at the sports centre.
Now listen again. What is right?

1 John Biggs is in:	2 They play:	3 It's:
a Liverpool	a 2 games	a 12 o'clock
b Manchester	b 5 games	b 2 o'clock
c Bristol.	c 10 games.	c 10 o'clock.

GRAMMAR

1 Verneinung mit *n't* und *don't:*

Die Verneinung englischer Sätze bilden Sie, indem Sie *n't* an den ersten Teil des Zeitworts/Verbs hängen. Weist der Satz nur ein Verb auf, so wird in der Verneinung *n't* an ein *do* angehängt, das Sie noch einsetzen müssen.

I **have got** my postcards. 1 2	I **haven't got** my postcards. 1 2
You **have got** a partner. 1 2	You **haven't got** a partner. 1 2
I **like** tennis. 1	I **don't like** tennis. 1 2
We **play** tennis. 1	We **don't play** tennis. 1 2
They **play** a lot. 1	They **don't play** a lot. 1 2

2 Fragen mit Fragewort und *do*:

In Step 2 leitete *do* als Signal die Frage in der Gegenwart ein. Vor dieses *do* kann auch ein Fragewort treten.

Where do you play?
When do you usually play?
Why do you ask?

3 Eigenschaftswörter:

Diese Wörter ermöglichen es uns, Dinge zu beschreiben und unseren Gefühlen Ausdruck zu verleihen. Damit werden unsere Aussagen für unsere Gesprächspartner griffiger und farbiger. Eigenschaftswörter können vor Hauptwörtern und mit dem Verb *be* benutzt werden.

a **new** restaurant	ein neues Restaurant
The restaurant is **new**.	Das Restaurant ist neu.

Die englischen Eigenschaftswörter bleiben dabei in ihrer Grundform erhalten und verändern sich im Gegensatz zum Deutschen nicht:

an **exciting** game	ein aufregendes Spiel
two **exciting** games	zwei aufregende Spiele

1 What do they say?

	T	M	C
play tennis	✓	✗	✓
work for the state	✗	✓	✗
work for an American firm	✗	✗	✓
like English beer	✓	✓	✗
drink coke	✓	✓	✓
eat hamburgers	✗	✓	✓

Make two sentences about Tina, Mark and Chris.
Example:
Tina: I play tennis.
I don't work for the state.

2 What is the right order?

A's questions are right, but B's answers are in the wrong order.

A: Do you like German food, Barbara?
B: Yes that's fine!
A: Good, and do you drink German beer?
B: Yes, I have but why do you ask?
A: Have you got time on Saturday?
B: No, I don't like beer.
A: Cambridge has got a new German restaurant.
B: Yes, I do. I like German food a lot.
A: It's next to the post office, opposite the Wessex bank. Let's go, on Saturday at 8.00 pm, Barbara. Is that OK?
B: Really? Where is it?

Now read the dialogue with your partner.

Lerntip

In diesem Kurs werden Sie oft dazu aufgefordert, etwas über sich selbst zu sagen. Dabei wollen wir nicht etwa in Ihre Privatsphäre eindringen, sondern realistische Situationen einüben, in denen Sie sich im Ausland oder mit ausländischen Besuchern befinden könnten. In diesem Step, zum Beispiel, wurden Sie darüber ausgefragt, was Sie gerne spielen. Im allgemeinen werden Sie wohl nichts dagegen haben, solche Fragen wahrheitsgemäß zu beantworten. (Wenn Ihnen dazu noch Vokabeln fehlen, fragen Sie Ihre Kursleiterin / Ihren Kursleiter.) Sollte Ihnen jedoch die eine oder andere Frage wirklich zu persönlich vorkommen, so können Sie natürlich ausweichend oder witzig antworten. Wie auch immer, versuchen Sie es auf englisch.

1 Please complete: where/do/don't/when.

A: ..... do you go to the pub, John?
B: I usually go on Saturday.
A: ..... do you go?
B: To the Bell Inn.
A: .....'s that?
B: It's that nice pub next to the museum.
A: ..... they close in the afternoon?
B: No, they ..... . They close at 11.30 pm.
A: Is the food good?
B: Yes, it's very good. I usually eat at the pub on Saturday.
A: I ..... like pub food.
B: But the food at the Bell Inn is great. Let's go to the Bell Inn on Saturday. It's really very nice.

2 Write the days of the week.

1 _ E _ _ _ _ _ _ _
2 _ _ U _ _ _ _ _
3 _ U _ _ _ _ _
4 _ O _ _ _ _
5 _ U _ _ _ _
6 _ _ I _ _ _
7 _ _ _ U _ _ _ _

3 Make sentences.

Peter and Susan are usually at the same place, at the same time, on the same day.

Monday	6.00	– tennis
Tuesday	8.00	– German class
Wednesday evening		– pub
Thursday evening		– disco
Friday	4.00	– squash
Saturday	11.00	– tennis
Sunday afternoon		– park

Make sentences like this:

They play tennis on Monday at 6 o'clock.
They go to a German class on Tuesday at 8 o'clock.

4 Make pairs.

1 next to	☐ a tennis
2 Sunday	☐ b drink
3 bank	☐ c exciting
4 eat	☐ d opposite
5 new	☐ e thank you
6 squash	☐ f post office
7 please	☐ g Friday

5 Say it in English. Please match.

Wie fragt man:

1 ob jemand Tennis spielt?
2 wann jemand Tennis spielt?
3 wo sie spielen?
4 ob sie Zeit am Wochenende haben?
5 ob 11 Uhr in Ordnung ist?

☐ a Have you got time at the weekend?
☐ b Is 11 o'clock OK?
☐ c Do you play tennis?
☐ d Where do you play?
☐ e When do you play tennis?

REVISION AND EXTENSION

• Starter

What time is it?
It's ...

1 Talk to your partner.

Example:
A: I like the camera.
B: That's £39.90.
...

2 A class questionnaire

Write five questions like this: Do you like ...?

biscuits beer gin sandwiches steaks
fish and chips whisky coffee ice-cream

Now ask three students your questions.
Example: – (Ingrid,) do you like (biscuits)?
– Yes, I do. / No, I don't.

Write the answers. ✔ = Yes, I do.
✘ = No, I don't.

Do you like biscuits?	Ingrid ✘ Richard ✔ Andy ✘

Heben Sie Ihren Fragebogen bitte auf. Sie brauchen ihn später wieder.

3 Where's the nearest ...?

pizzeria	delicatessen	bank	pub

Penn Street

post office	supermarket	museum	disco

Ask your partner five questions.

Example:
– Where's the nearest delicatessen?
– It's in Penn Street, opposite the supermarket.

REVISION AND EXTENSION

4 And now you.

Ask and answer questions about your city/place.
Example:
– Where's the nearest (post office)?
– It's in ...
It's next to ...
It's opposite ...

5 Game: Buzz

Zählen Sie. Jedesmal wenn eine Zahl etwas mit 7 zu tun hat, sagen Sie 'buzz'. Vergessen Sie, 'buzz' zu sagen, setzen Sie eine Runde aus.

Start like this: 1 - 2 - 3 - 4 - 5 - 6 - buzz - 8 - 9 ...

Denken Sie daran: auch 14 (2 mal 7), 27, 28 (4 mal 7) und 63 sind 'buzz'.

6 Memory check

Welche Wörter fallen Ihnen spontan ein, die Sie in Unit 3 gelernt haben? Schreiben Sie sie auf und vergleichen Sie Ihre Liste mit der Ihres Nachbarn / Ihrer Nachbarin.

7 Reading

In England banks open between 9.00 am and 10 am and they close between 3.30 pm and 4.30 pm. A lot of pubs still open at 10.30 in the morning and close at 2.30 in the afternoon. Then they open again in the afternoon and close at 11 o'clock in the evening. But pubs are also open all day now. Restaurants usually close at 11.30 pm and discos close at 2.00 am.

Shops usually open at 9.00 am and close at 5 or 5.30 pm. Corner shops often open at 9 or 10 o'clock in the morning and close at 10 or 11 o'clock in the evening. They open all week. On Sunday, too! The owners are often immigrants from Pakistan or India.

Option:

Write about shops, banks etc in your country and your town. Write to your teacher.

• Useful phrases

UNIT 4

People and plans

LONDON TRANSPORT MUSEUM

Unit 4

Begegnungen und Pläne. Das Nachbarehepaar Wilson berichtet Tina über den Sohn, der "fliegender Arzt" in Australien ist. Wir erfahren den ungewöhnlichen Tagesablauf einer schwedischen Nachrichtensprecherin, die bei Helen zu Gast ist. Tina und Mark machen Pläne für einen Ausflug nach London. In dieser Unit lernen Sie u.a.:

- Gewohnheiten und Tagesabläufe beschreiben
- Vorschläge machen
- Reiseverbindungen und -zeiten erfragen.

STEP 1

The neighbours

STARTER

What languages or dialects do you speak?
What languages or dialects do you understand?

I speak ...

I speak a bit of ...

I understand ...

I don't speak ... but I understand ...

I understand a bit of ...

DIALOGUE

Part 1

(Mrs W = Mrs Wilson)

Mrs W: Look Tina! I've got a postcard here from Terry.
Tina: That's nice. Does he often write?
Mrs W: Yes, he does. Very often ... He lives in Alice Springs now with his Japanese wife.
Tina: A Japanese wife? Does he speak Japanese?
Mrs W: No, he doesn't. He understands a bit but his wife speaks English. Her English is very good.

Part 2

Mark: Who's Terry?
Tina: He's their son. He's a flying doctor in Australia.
Mark: Oh, really, that's interesting.
Tina: Yes, he likes it, the weather is great ... oh no ... Mark, let's have our next summer holiday in Australia.
Mark: Tina, our summer is their winter!

ACTIVITIES

Part 1

1a Talk about Terry's wife, Midori.

Example: She often eats Japanese food.

work drink play write eat speak live

coffee Japanese food books at home squash Alice Springs Japanese English

1b And now you.

Write down five questions. Then ask another student. Here are seven ideas:

like? live? eat? speak? play? drink? work?

Now tell the class about your partner:
He/She lives in ...

1c Answer questions about Terry.

With your partner answer the questions.
Say/Write *Yes, he does / No, he doesn't.*

1 Does he often write to his mother?
2 Does he live in London?
3 Does he like Australia?
4 Does he speak Japanese?
5 Does he understand a bit of Japanese?

1d Ask your teacher.

Teacher: This is my father/sister/friend/...
You: Does he/she ...?

like ...? eat ...? live in ...?
understand Japanese ...? work for ...?
play ...? speak English ...? drink ...?

And now ask your partner.

A: This is my ...
B: Does he/she ...
A: Yes, he/she does. / No, he/she doesn't.

Part 2

2a Our postcard or their postcard?

Die Hälfte der Klasse war im Urlaub in den USA und die andere Hälfte in Großbritannien. Nun wollen Sie alle gemeinsam Ihre Mitbringsel anschauen. Leider sind die Sachen etwas durcheinander gekommen. Teilen Sie sie wieder auf.

Example:
The postcard of London is our postcard.
The map of New York is their map.

Listening & pronunciation

3a Listen again.

Listen to the dialogue parts 1-2 again.

3b Listen and repeat: [dʒ]

Listen to 'cheers' [tʃ] and 'German' [dʒ]. Now say the words with [dʒ]:

Japanese	Germany	orange
Japan	John	
German	sandwich	

3c Listen and answer.

Midori is in Japan. Listen to the dialogue.
Now read the questions and listen to the dialogue again.
Now answer the questions.

1 Does he speak Japanese?
2 Does Midori say "your English is good"?
3 Does the man work in Japan?

GRAMMAR

1 Wie Sie Aussagen in der 3. Person Gegenwart machen:

Die Bildung von Aussagen und Fragen mit *I*, *you*, *we*, *they* haben Sie in Unit 3 kennengelernt. Wird von einer dritten Person (er, sie, es) gesprochen (z.B. *Terry*, *Tina*, *he*, *she*, *the pub*), wird dem Zeitwort/Verb ein s hinzugefügt.

He	live**s** in Alice Springs now.
He	understand**s** a bit.
His wife/She	speak**s** English.
The pub	close**s** at 3 o'clock.

-es wird als Sonderfall in der 3. Person Einzahl an *do* und *go* gehängt: **does** [dʌz], **goes** [gəʊz].

2 Fragen mit *does:*

Das System der Bildung einer Frage, das Sie aus Unit 3 kennen, bleibt natürlich auch in der 3. Person Einzahl erhalten, nur müssen Sie darauf achten, die Verbform *does* zu verwenden:

Does he often write?
Does he speak Japanese?
Does she work in Australia?
Does it close at 3 o'clock?

Diese Regel gilt selbstverständlich auch für Fragen, die mit einem Fragewort beginnen:

What does he ask?
Where does she work?
When does it close?

3 Kurzantworten mit *does:*

Bei Kurzantworten nehmen Sie wie gewohnt das *does* der Frage in Ihrer Antwort nach *yes* oder *no* wieder auf:

Fragen	Kurzantworten
Does he live here?	Yes, he **does**. No, he **doesn't.**
Does Midori say ...?	Yes, she **does**. No, she **doesn't**.
Does it close ...?	Yes, it **does**. No, it **doesn't**.

1 Please answer the questions.

Janice Keenan:
- works for an American firm now
- lives near London
- speaks and writes German
- understands Japanese
- likes sports
- reads a lot of books.

1 Does Janice Keenan work for a Japanese firm now?
2 Does she live in London?
3 Does she speak Japanese?
4 Does she write Japanese?
5 Does she speak German?
6 Does she write German?
7 Does she like sports?

2 Please complete Mark's questions.

Mark asks Tina about Terry and his Japanese wife.

M: he / live / in Australia?
Does he live in Australia?
T: Yes, he lives in Alice Springs. He's a flying doctor.
M: he / like it?
T: Yes, he does.
M: he / often / write?
T: Yes, very often.
M: his wife / speak / English?
T: Yes, her English is good.
M: he / understand / Japanese?
T: A bit.
M: she / like / Australia?
T: Yes, she likes Australia a lot.

HOMESTUDY

Lerntip

Bei der Partner- und Kleingruppenarbeit im Unterricht sollten Sie darauf achten, daß Sie mit möglichst vielen verschiedenen Kursmitgliedern arbeiten, denn so können Sie sich untereinander am besten beim Lernen helfen. Immer mit demselben Partner zu üben ist nicht nur weniger interessant, Sie laufen auch Gefahr, voneinander die Fehler zu lernen, was nicht so leicht passiert, wenn Sie nach und nach mit jedem/jeder üben. Und lassen Sie sich nicht entmutigen, wenn Sie meinen, daß einige in der Gruppe besser oder schneller lernen als Sie. Es geht gar nicht darum, eine Reihenfolge aufzustellen, sondern sich gegenseitig beim Lernen zu unterstützen.

1 Please complete.

This is the postcard from Terry to his mother. Complete the postcard with: lives, works, goes, likes, eats, speaks.

Dear Mum + Dad,
Midori and I are on holiday in Japan. We are in Osaka with her family. They are very nice. Midori's father ... for a computer firm and her brother is a student. He ... in Tokyo. I don't understand Japanese, but Midori's mother ... English. She ... to English classes. We don't eat Japanese food in Australia but Midori ... Japanese food very much and she is very happy here. She ... a lot!
Love,
Terry and Midori

2 Write the answers: Yes, he/she does. / No, he/she doesn't.

1 Does Midori's father work for a computer firm?
2 Does Midori's mother speak English?
3 Does Terry understand Japanese?
4 Does Midori eat Japanese food in Australia?
5 Does Midori's brother live in Tokyo?

3 What do they say?

our daughter lives in Australia
our son lives in Tokyo
our daughter's name is Vanessa
our son lives in Australia
our son's name is John
our son is a flying doctor

1 Mr and Mrs Wilson say their son ...
2 Mr and Mrs Wilson say their ...
3 Helen and Norman say ...
4 Helen and Norman say ...
5 Mr and Mrs Hokiado say ...
6 Mr and Mrs Hokiado say ...

4 Say it in English. Please match.

Was sagen Sie, wenn Sie wissen wollen, ob jemand

1 Australien mag?	a ☐ Does he/she speak Japanese?
2 Japanisch spricht?	b ☐ Does he/she play tennis?
3 Tennis spielt?	c ☐ Does he/she eat Japanese food?
4 für den Staat arbeitet?	d ☐ Does he/she like Australia?
5 japanisches Essen ißt?	e ☐ Does he/she work for the state?

STEP 2

Small talk

STARTER

1 Revision

Your teacher thinks of a person in this book (Midori, Terry, Tina, ...). Who is it? Ask questions with *does*.
Example:
– Does he/she live (in England)?
– Yes, he/she does. / No, he/she doesn't.
...
– Is it (Midori)?
–Yes, it is. / No, it isn't.

live like speak
drink
understand work for
eat

2 Vocabulary. Norman's day.

This is what Norman does every day.
Match the sentences and the pictures.

1 He goes to bed at 10.00.
2 He eats Cornflakes for breakfast.
3 He starts work at 8.00.
4 Norman gets up at 6.00.
5 He reads the newspaper.
6 He comes home at 5.00.

DIALOGUE

Part 1

(H = Helen, S = Sven Olsen)

S: Good morning. I'm sorry I'm a bit late for breakfast.
H: Eight o'clock, that's not late!
S: Oh, but at home my wife always gets up at 4.30.
H: 4.30? That's very early.
S: Yes, she works for a Swedish radio station. She reads the early morning news.
H: That's interesting. Do you get up early, too?
S: Yes, sometimes.

Part 2

(A = Astrid Olsen)

H: Your wife must be very tired in the evening.
S: Oh, she doesn't work in the afternoon. She always comes home at 2 o' clock and she doesn't go to bed very late.
A: Oh, am I late for breakfast? It's 8 o' clock ...
S: Astrid, this is England, and we're on holiday now! (→ *Andere Länder, andere Sitten*)

ACTIVITIES

Part 1

1a Ask your partner about his/her day.

Write down your questions.
Example: When do you get up?

when? — get up — go to bed — start work — come home

what? — drink for breakfast — eat for breakfast

Now ask your partner. Then tell the class about your partner.

1b Exchange information with your partner.

A: look at this page. B: look at page 112.
A: Look at the box, ask your partner questions like this: How often do you …?

	never	sometimes	often	usually	always
drink tea for breakfast					
get up at 6.00					
speak English					
go to bed late					
write postcards on holiday					
eat toast for breakfast					
go to a disco					

Now tell the class about your partner. Example: (Peter) often drinks coffee for breakfast.

Part 2

2a Talk about Astrid.

She …
She doesn't …

2b Talk about Norman.

Look at the starter on page 66 and activity 2a on page 55. Say three positive and three negative sentences.

like — play — drink — eat — work — live — get up — start work — go to — read — come home — speak

Example:
Norman lives in King's Lynn.
He doesn't work at home.
He gets up at …

Listening & pronunciation

3a Listen again.

Listen to the dialogue parts 1-2 again.

3b Listen and repeat: [əʊ] – [ɒ]

[əʊ]	[ɒ]	[əʊ]	[ɒ]
so	problem	post office	coffee
go	got	OK	along
know	not	video	a lot
oh	shop	coke	opposite
postcard	holiday	phone	sorry

Now say this:
I know you go to the disco.
I've got a lot of problems.
The photo shop opposite the post office closes at five o'clock.

3c Listen and answer.

Norman speaks about Helen's day. True or false?

1 Norman's wife doesn't work a lot.
2 She gets up early.
3 She usually gets up at 7.30.
4 Breakfast is from 7.00 - 9.00.
5 Helen goes to the shops at 11.00.

GRAMMAR

1 Verneinung mit *doesn't*:

Die Verneinungsregel aus Unit 3 bleibt auch für die 3. Person Einzahl gültig, so daß sich das folgende Muster ergibt:

Aussage	Verneinte Aussage
She **reads** the newspaper. 1	She **doesn't read** the newspaper. 1 2
He **plays** golf. 1	He **doesn't play** golf. 1 2
He **goes** to work. 1	He **doesn't go** to work. 1 2

Bitte achten Sie darauf, daß das *-s* oder *-es* grundsätzlich nur einmal angehängt wird und zwar an das erste Verb bzw. den ersten Verbteil.

2 Wo Sie *always/usually/often/sometimes/never* im Satz stellen:

She **usually** gets up at 7.30. She **often** drinks tea.	Diese Wörter stehen vor dem Verb.
She's **never** late.	Aber nach dem Verb *be*.

Die Stellung dieser Wörter, die so ganz anders als im Deutschen ist, wird sich Ihnen durch den häufigen Gebrauch ganz automatisch einprägen.

1 Write about Sven.

	never	sometimes	often	usually	always
get up at 4.30		✓			
drink tea			✓		
go to work early					✓
work late				✓	
play tennis	✓				
read a newspaper				✓	

Astrid's husband sometimes gets up at 4.30 in the morning. He...

2 Don't or doesn't?

1 Astrid ..... work in the afternoon.
2 She gets up early and ..... go to bed late.
3 Astrid and Sven ..... usually get up early on Saturday.
4 They ..... work at the weekends.
5 Astrid likes bed-and-breakfast places, but she ..... like hotels.
6 She and her husband ..... usually go to hotels when they come to England on holiday.

3 And now you.

Write about a friend or a person in your family.

– He/She doesn't like coffee. He/She doesn't ...
+ He/She likes tea. He/She ...

HOMESTUDY

Lerntip

Das Schreiben auf englisch mag zunächst etwas mühsam sein, aber geben Sie nicht auf. Natürlich werden Sie von Ihrem ersten Entwurf nicht immer entzückt sein – das ist völlig normal. (Was meinen Sie, wie oft wir diesen Absatz umgeändert haben, bis wir mit ihm halbwegs zufrieden waren?) Nehmen Sie sich etwas Zeit, machen Sie sich ein paar Notizen, schreiben Sie einen ersten Entwurf, schlagen Sie hier im Lehrbuch nach, wenn Sie unsicher sind, ändern Sie um – und dann erst schreiben Sie Ihre endgültige Fassung ab. Und vor allem: schreiben Sie von vornherein auf englisch. Übersetzen ist viel schwieriger und verleitet zu unnötigen Fehlern.

1 Please complete.

Astrid Lindstrom (live) in Uppsala with her husband and two daughters. She (work) for a radio station where she (read) the news. She (start) work at 6.00. She (speak) English but she (not speak) German. She (get up) very early, at 4.30, but she (not work) in the afternoons.
At the weekend she (not read) the news; she is at home with her family. She (like) tennis and usually (play) with her daughter on Saturday afternoons. Her husband (not play) tennis but he (like) ice-hockey.
This summer she is in England on holiday with her husband. She often (go) to England. She (like) bed-and-breakfast places, but she (not like) hotels. (→ *Andere Länder, andere Sitten*)

2 Odd man out.

1 when, why, where, (weather)
2 sometimes, never, always, early
3 Monday, weekend, Wednesday, Friday
4 at, too, in, on
5 understand, get up, read, speak
6 wife, husband, sister, friend
7 pub, museum, street, restaurant

3 What is the right order?

1 It's at nine o'clock
2 Oh, that's very early. Why so early?
3 That's OK. You're not late.

(A = Astrid, H = Helen)
A: I'm sorry I'm a bit late for breakfast.
H: ...
A: When is breakfast?
H: ...
A: In Sweden I usually eat breakfast at 5 o'clock.
H: ...
A: I read the early morning news on the radio.

4 Say it in English.

Sie möchten wissen, ob Astrid:

1 viel arbeitet
2 am Wochenende arbeitet
3 die Nachrichten liest
4 früh aufsteht
5 spät ins Bett geht
6 Deutsch spricht

Does she ...?
Does ...
...

STEP 3

At tourist information

STARTER

1 Revision

What do you remember about the other students and the teacher?

Example:
(Sabine) likes dogs.
(Peter) often gets up early.
(Alex) doesn't speak Japanese.

2 Vocabulary

Please match.

1 coach 2 plane 3 bike 4 train 5 car

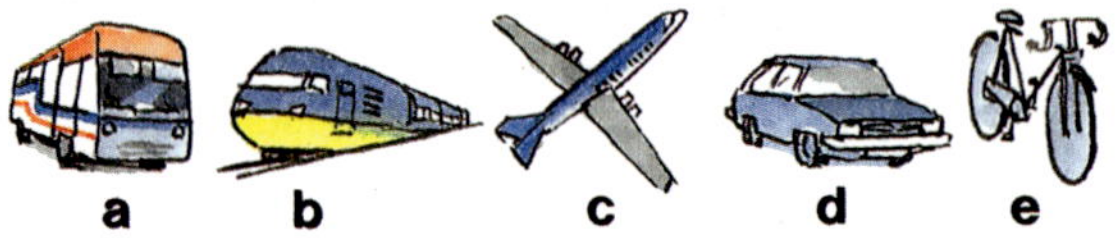

a b c d e

DIALOGUE

Part 1

Tina: OK. Where would you like to go? Cambridge or London?
Mark: Well, I'd like to go to the London Transport Museum.
Tina: Oh, you and your trains, Mark. – OK, the transport museum in the morning but I'd like to go to Docklands in the afternoon. – How would you like to go: by train or by coach?
Mark: By train of course! – When does the museum open?
Tina: I don't know. Let's go to the tourist information office in Bridge Street.

Part 2

Tina: Excuse me. When does the London Transport Museum open?
Clerk: One moment, please. It opens at 10.00 and closes at 6.00.
Mark: Oh, let's go early.
Tina: How early? We're on holiday.
Mark: When does the first train leave?
Clerk: At 6.15.
Tina: Oh no, that's too early.
Clerk: The next train leaves at 7.30.
Tina: And what time does it arrive?
Clerk: At 9.05.
T+M: Thank you. Goodbye.

ACTIVITIES

Part 1

1a Ask your teacher.

1 How do you go to work?
2 How do you come to the English class?
3 How do you go to the shops?
4 How do you go on holiday?
5 How do you go to the bank?

Now ask your partner. Here are five ideas for your answers.

by train by car by bus
by bike I walk

Example:
– How do you come to the English class?
– I usually come by bike, but I sometimes walk.

1b What would you like to see in London?

You are in London. Talk in a group like this:

A: I'd like to go to Buckingham Palace.
B: Yes, that's a good idea.
C: Oh, no, I'd like to go to the London Docklands.

Part 2

2a Exchange information with your partner.

A: look at this page. B: look at page 113.
A: You are a tourist in London. B works for the tourist information office. He/She answers your questions. Example:

A: When does the British Museum open?
B: It opens at 10.00 am.
A: When does it close?
B: It closes at 5.00 pm.

British Museum	
Madame Tussauds	
London Transport Museum	
Wimbledon Tennis Museum	
Houses of Parliament	
Tower of London	

2b Ask your partner.

London – Athens	12.05 – 17.45
London – Rome	17.25 – 20.55
London – Bangkok	14.00 – 07.55
London – Tel Aviv	16.50 – 23.25
London – Munich	08.15 – 11.00

Example: A: I'd like to go to (Bangkok).
When does the plane leave?
B: It leaves at (2 pm).
A: And when does it arrive?
B: It arrives at (7.55 am).

Listening & pronunciation

3a Listen again.

Listen to the dialogue Parts 1-2 again.

3b Listen and repeat: [r].

Der Buchstabe 'r' wird im Englischen nicht immer ausgesprochen, besonders im britischen Englisch. In diesen Wortpaaren wird das 'r' im zweiten Wort jeweils nicht ausgesprochen.

Austria	German	radio	computer
very	early	train	car
tourist	first	arrive	there
drink	beer	friend	father
read	work	Friday	Thursday

Now say this:
Here's your beer. Cheers!
The early morning train arrives at four thirty.
I never read newspapers in the afternoon.

3c Listen and answer.

Listen to the dialogue at the tourist information office. Are the sentences true or false?

1 She'd like to go to Bath.
2 She'd like to go by train.
3 She'd like to go in the morning.
4 The first train leaves at 7.20.
5 It arrives at 7.30.

GRAMMAR

1 Wie Sie Fragewörter *What/When/Where/How/Why* mit *does* benutzen:

Nachdem Sie etwas Sicherheit im Umgang mit Fragesätzen gewonnen haben, können Sie Fragewörter nunmehr in vielen Alltagssituationen verwenden.

What	**does** Mark like?	was?
When	**does** he go to work?	wann?
Where	**does** he live?	wo?
Where	**does** he go?	wohin?
Why	**does** he go by train?	warum?
How	**does** he go there?	wie?

2 Wie Sie ausdrücken, daß Sie etwas tun möchten:

I **would** / I'**d like** to go to Docklands.	Ich möchte ...
We **would** / We'**d like** to go to the new museum.	Wir möchten ...
Where **would** you **like** to go?	Wohin möchtest Du / möchten Sie ...?
How w**ould** you **like** to go?	Wie möchtest Du / möchten Sie ...?

Questions, questions, questions

This is a memory quiz. What do you remember?

1 Who is Helen's daughter?
2 What is Helen's husband's name?
3 Where is Helen from?
4 Have Karen and Paul got a photo of Hamburg?
5 Who is Tina's brother?
6 What's the name of the pub near the bed-and-breakfast?
7 How much is the map of King's Lynn in the shop?
8 Does Chris like English beer?
9 Does Mark like tennis?
10 Where does Terry live?
11 When does Astrid get up?
12 Where would Mark like to go?

Tip: the questions are in the order of the Units and Steps. (Question 1 is from Unit 1 Step 1, etc).

1 Ask questions.

Post Office	9.00 am – 5.30 pm
Tourist Office	8.30 am – 6.00 pm
British Museum	10.00 am – 5.00 pm
Banks	9.45 am – 3.30 pm
Shops	9.00 am – 5.30 pm
The Bridge Restaurant	11.30 am – 11.00 pm

1 When does the post office open? – It opens at 9.00 am.
2 ... – It closes at 11.00 pm.
3 ... – It opens at 8.30 am.
4 ... – They close at 3.30 pm.
5 ... – It opens at 10.00 am.
6 ... – They close at 5.30 pm.

2 And now you.

Write about places in your town. Write four sentences.

bank
post office supermarket
museum restaurant

3 Please complete with would like / 'd like

A: (I) to go to Paris, please.
B: How (you) like to go?
A: Well, (I) to be in Paris at 4 pm.
B: (You) to go by bus or by train?
A: I think (I) to go by plane.

Lerntip

Beim Sprachenlernen ist Wiederholen und Festigen fast genauso wichtig wie Weiterlernen. Deshalb haben wir Sie in dieser Lektion gebeten, Fragen auch über den Inhalt der vorangegangenen Lektionen zu beantworten. Dabei mußten Sie etwas suchen und wurden an früher gelernte Wörter und Strukturen erinnert. Legen Sie von sich aus immer wieder kleine Wiederholungsphasen ein, Sie werden dadurch sicherer in Ihrem Sprachgebrauch.

1 Ask questions.

Mrs Wilson and Mark talk about Tina. What does Mrs Wilson ask?

(W = Mrs Wilson, M = Mark)
W: where/work? = Where does she work?
M: She works for an international firm in Hamburg.
W: when/start work?
M: At 8 o'clock.
W: Oh that's early. when/get up?
M: She usually gets up at six thirty.
W: what time/come home?
M: Usually at seven in the evening.
W: That's late. how/come home?
M: She comes home by car. The office isn't very near where we live.

2 Please complete: to/by/for/on/in/with/from.

Dear Jessica and Mike,
I'm ... holiday ... Paris ... Cathy.
The weather is very nice. ... the morning we usually go ... bus to the city centre to see the interesting places. ... Saturday afternoon we'd like to go ... Versailles.
Love, David
PS: Thank you ... your postcard ... Wales.

3 Please complete.

The text helps you to complete the crossword.

John and Wendy would like to go 6) t... Edinburgh 4) n... weekend. They'd like to go by 3) t... . It 1) l... London at 9.00 am and arrives 7) i... Edinburgh at 2.00 pm. John would like to go to a 2) h... near the station but Wendy would like to go to a bed-and-breakfast. This is their first 5) h... in Scotland!

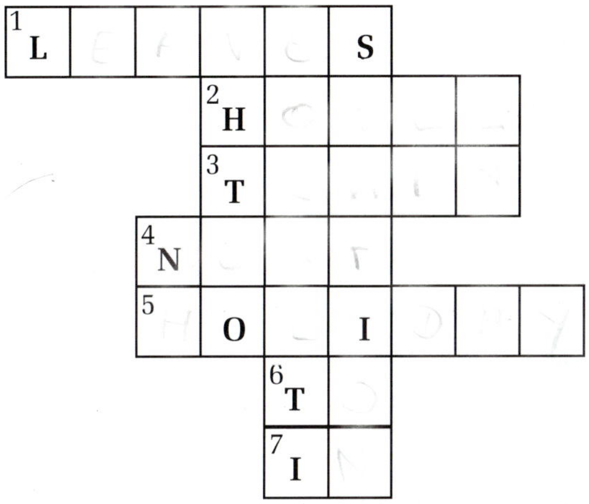

4 Say it in English.

Was sagen Sie, wenn:

1 Sie etwas nicht wissen?
2 Jemand kurz warten soll?
3 Sie sich verabschieden und bedanken wollen?
4 Etwas zu früh ist?
5 Sie jemanden ansprechen, um etwas zu fragen?

a ☐ It's too early.
b ☐ I'm sorry, I don't know.
c ☐ Excuse me.
d ☐ Goodbye and thank you.
e ☐ One moment, please.

REVISION AND EXTENSION

• Starter

Ask your teacher questions with *often/sometimes* like this:

– Do you often play tennis?
Do you sometimes ...?

1 Please match.

1 Do you like the food in Japan?
2 Does Charles live in Australia?
3 Do Danny and Jane work for a bank?
4 Do you and your friend often go to Scotland?
5 Does Susan play badminton?

☐ a No, he doesn't.
☐ b Yes, we do.
☐ c No, they don't.
☐ d No, she doesn't.
☐ e Yes, I do.

Now say the questions and answers with your partner.

2 Your class list

Look at your class questionnaire in Revision and Extension p. 58.

Now tell your class about the three students.

Example: Ingrid and Andy don't like biscuits but Richard likes biscuits....

3 What's the right order?

Find the days of the week.

1 YSDANU *Sunday*
2 DUYASTE ...
3 IADRYF ...
4 OANMYD ...
5 RUTAYDAS ...
6 YADRUSTH ...

4 Please complete.

Christel and Dave ..... (live) in Newcastle. Christel ..... (work) at Newcastle College. She's a teacher. Dave ..... (be) a restaurant manager.

Christel and Dave ..... (get up) early. They ..... (have) breakfast at 7 o'clock. Christel ..... (leave) the house at 8 o'clock. Then Dave ..... (read) the newspaper before he ..... (go) to work. He ..... (work) in a pizzeria. He ..... (start) work at 10 am and ..... (come) home at 3.00 pm. Then he ..... (start) work again at 5.30 pm. Christel ..... (not work) in the evening. She often ..... (meet) friends in the evening. In winter Christel usually ..... (go) to bed early.

5 And now you.

Tell your partner about a typical day.
Start like this:

I usually get up at ... Then I ...

6 Ask questions.

Work in groups of four students. Ask and answer questions.

Example: Do you play tennis?

Yes, I do.	No, I don't.
I often play tennis. I always play tennis on Wednesday. I often play tennis in summer. I never play tennis in winter. I sometimes play tennis with my boyfriend.	I don't like tennis. Tennis is not very interesting. I think tennis is awful. ...

1 Do you read a lot?
2 Do you like breakfast?
3 Do you get up early?
4 Do you live here in ...?
5 Do you ...

REVISION AND EXTENSION

7 Question and answer tennis

Machen Sie einen Papierball. Wählen Sie ein Fragewort (What? Where? How? Who?). Sagen Sie es und werfen Sie jemandem den Ball zu. Er/Sie muß eine Frage mit Ihrem Fragewort bilden und den Ball weiterwerfen. Der/Die nächste gibt eine Antwort und 'wirft' ein neues Fragewort, usw. Wem keine Frage oder Antwort einfällt, setzt eine Runde aus.

8 Memory check

Welche Wörter fallen Ihnen spontan ein, die Sie in Unit 4 gelernt haben? Schreiben Sie sie auf und vergleichen Sie Ihre Liste mit der Ihres Nachbarn / Ihrer Nachbarin.

9 Reading

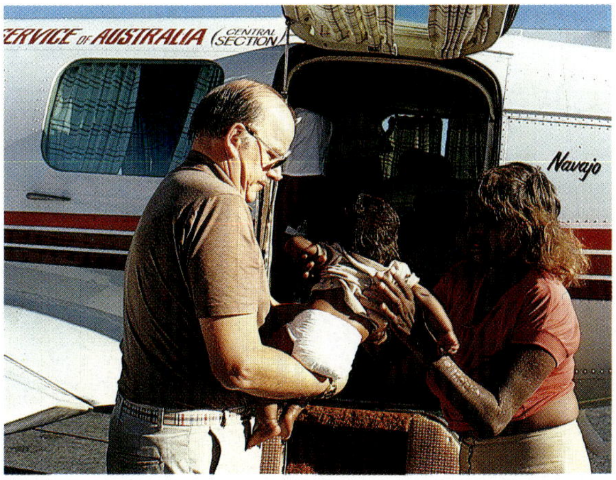

Terry is from England but he now lives and works in Alice Springs in Australia. He is a flying doctor. He usually leaves the house early and goes to the medical centre where he works. His patients do not come to Alice Springs – he flies out to see his patients in a plane. The patients live in the 'outback', sometimes 400 or 500 miles from the medical centre. In an emergency Terry sometimes operates on his patients in the plane, or he flies his patient to the nearest hospital.
Terry likes his work. He thinks it's very hard but very interesting.

Option:
Do you know someone with an interesting job? Write about the person and the job. Ask your teacher for help.

• Useful phrases

Extra 2

Song

By train

Listen and complete.

Two men, ... jobs
They both ..... work at nine
One man always gets there .....
But the other man's ..... on time:

'I always ..... my home at eight
And I always ..... at nine
In the ..... sun and the ..... rain
I always go to work by .....
I always go by .....'

Two men, ... jobs
They both ..... work at nine
One man always goes by .....
But he's ..... there on time.
His boss says, 'Why don't you ..... try
To get to ..... on time?'

(And the other man says)
'I always ..... my home at eight
And I always ..... at nine
In the ..... sun and the ..... rain
I always go to work by .....
I always go by ..... I always
No, not ..... go by .....'

Crossword

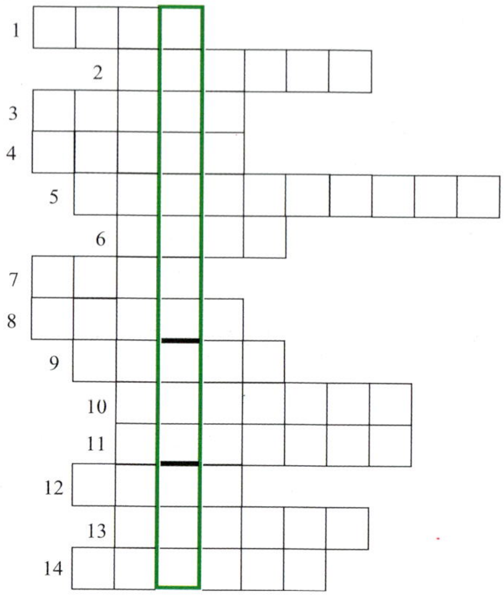

1 She lives there ..... her husband.
2 Terry is a flying ..... in Australia.
3 I get up at 6 o'clock. – That's very ..... .
4 My husband goes to work by ..... .
5 Do you ..... Japanese?
6 Let's ..... in the park.
7 Does your girlfriend ..... tennis, too?
8 When do shops ..... in England?
9 I've got a postcard, but I haven't got a ..... .
10 The train leaves London at 10.15 am and ..... in Bristol at 12.35 pm.
11 Excuse me. Where's the ..... post office, please?
12 Go along Bridge Street, then turn ..... .
13 The day before Monday is ..... .
14 I like summer but I don't like ..... .

The mystery sentence is: _ _ _ _ _ _ _ _ _ _ _ _ _ _.

words with 's'

How many words can you find that start with an 's'? You have got one minute. Write the words down.

Sunday, sometimes...

Now make sentences and talk to your partner. Use one 's' word in your sentence. Example:

On Sundays I get up late.

Spotlight

Australia and the Olgas.

The Ayers Rock - Mt Olga National Park is 450 kilometres away from Alice Springs. Ayers Rock and the Olgas are mountains in a part of Australia with a lot of red sand but not a lot of vegetation and with no houses. But they are very exciting and interesting because they have got faces and because there are a lot of symbols and paintings. The paintings tell us a lot about the aborigines, the first people in Australia, and so the Olgas are a big attraction for tourists.

On the way from Alice Springs to the Olgas is the Virginia Camel Farm. You can go on a camel safari from there. But a safari in the day is not always a good idea. In summer, that's our winter, it is sometimes +44° C in the middle of the day (at 12 or 1 pm).

Games & puzzles

Chain game

Say the sentences again and add something new.

A: I like tea.
B: I like tea in the morning.
C: I sometimes like tea in the morning.
D: I...
E: I...

How many sentences can you make?

What's my name ?

1 I'm from Austria.
I live in America.
You can see me on TV.
I'm a film star.
I'm a man.

2 My home is in Paris.
I'm in a museum.
A lot of people come to see me.
I always smile.
I'm a woman.

Who is 00 Buzz?

Can you remember the game 'Buzz' (p. 59)?

Who is 00 Buzz? –
It's _ _ _ _ _ _ _ _ _ _.

Sightseeing

The river and university in Cambridge

The London Docklands

Big Ben and the Houses of Parliament

Unit 5

Reiseberichte stehen im Mittelpunkt. Helens Gast aus Schweden berichtet über einen Ausflug nach Cambridge. John erhält einen Brief von Freunden, die eine Reise nach Kanada gemacht haben. Tina und Mark laden Chris zum Abendessen ein und berichten über ihren Ausflug nach London.

In dieser Unit lernen Sie, wie man über die Vergangenheit spricht.

STEP 1

What was your day like?

STARTER

Ask your teacher.

Ask your teacher where he/she was yesterday.
Examples:
Were you at home?
Were you at a restaurant?
Were you at a tourist information office?
Were you ...?

at home • at the office
at a tourist information office
at the bank • at the sports centre
at the post office • at the shops
at a museum • at a disco • at a hotel
at a pub • at a restaurant in (Scotland)
at work • in (London) • on holiday

DIALOGUE

Part 1

(S = Sven, K = Karel, a Czech tourist)

S: ... and where were you yesterday?
K: I was in Colchester.
S: Oh, what was it like?
K: Colchester was interesting, but the weather was awful. I was in a museum all day, and I had a nice meal there. And you?
S: I was in Cambridge.
K: Oh, yes, and was the weather awful there, too?
S: No, it wasn't. It was very nice.

Part 2

K: And was your wife with you?
S: No, Astrid wasn't very well. She was in bed all day. But she was OK in the evening.
K: That's good.
S: But I wasn't very well in the evening.
K: Oh, why was that?
S: Well, I was in Cambridge with Vanessa, and we were in a punt on the river.
K: A punt? What's that?
S: It's a kind of boat. It was my first time in a punt. Suddenly, I don't know how ... I was in the water ...

ACTIVITIES

Part 1

1a Where were you?

WHERE'S DUDLEY?
Yesterday one of the Queen's dogs, Dudley, a five-year-old

Your teacher is a detective. You are one of the Royal Family. Your teacher asks you questions.

Example:
T: Dudley was here in the morning but he wasn't here at 3.00 pm. Where were you at 3.00 pm yesterday?
You: I was (at a museum in London).

Look at the starter for ideas.

1b Find someone who ...

Where were you on Monday evening and Wednesday morning? Answer the questions.

	Names
On Monday evening I was ...	
On Wednesday morning I was ...	

Who was there too?
Ask the other students like this:
– Were you ... on Monday evening?
– Yes, I was. / No, I wasn't.
– Were you ... on Wednesday morning?
– Yes, I was. / No, I wasn't.

Who says 'Yes, I was.'? Write down the names.

Part 2

2a Please answer the questions.

1 Where was Karel yesterday?
2 What was the weather like in Colchester?
3 Where was Astrid yesterday?
4 Where were Vanessa and Sven yesterday?
5 Where were you yesterday?
6 Where were you and your friend/dog/...?

2b Exchange information with your partner.

A: look at this page. B: look at page 113.

A: you and B organised an international party on Saturday. But where were the guests? It wasn't the right day! Now it's Monday. Ask B questions and answer B's questions.

Vanessa	?
Helen	at the shops
Norman	at the sports centre
John	?
Karel	on the river
Astrid + Sven	?
the Wilsons	in Cambridge
Tina + Mark	?

Example: A: Where was (Vanessa)?
B: (She was with a friend in Norwich).

Listening & pronunciation

3a Listen again.

Listen to the dialogue parts 1-2 again.

3b Listen and repeat: [w]

well	**w**elcome	**w**ith	**w**ere	**w**here
weather	**w**ife	**w**ater	**w**e	**w**hen

Where was Vanessa? Was she in Wales?
No, she wasn't but we were there.
When were you in Wales?
We were there at the weekend.

3c Listen and answer.

Anna asks Barbara about her holiday. Listen and answer the questions.

1 Where was Barbara on holiday?
2 When was she there?
3 What was the weather like?

GRAMMAR

1 Wie Sie über die Vergangenheit sprechen:

Sprechen wir im Englischen über etwas Vergangenes und Abgeschlossenes, müssen wir die Zeitform der Vergangenheit benutzen. Im Deutschen sind wir nicht so gebunden und können auch das Perfekt ("Ich bin in Colchester gewesen und habe dort das Museum besucht.") gebrauchen; nicht so im Englischen.

2 *Was/Were.* Aussagesätze mit dem Verb *be* in der Vergangenheit:

I	**was** in Colchester.
You	**were** in Cambridge.
He/She	**was** in London.
It	**was** fine.
We	**were** in bed all day.
You	**were** in a punt on the river.
They	**were** well.

3 *Wasn't/Weren't.* Verneinte Aussagesätze mit dem Verb *be* in der Vergangenheit:

Sie verneinen Aussagen mit *was* und *were* ganz einfach, indem Sie *n't* direkt an die Verbform hängen oder das Wort *not* nachstellen wie im Deutschen.

I **wasn't / was not** in London.
You **weren't / were not** there at the weekend.

4 Fragesätze mit *was* und *were:*

Das Ihnen geläufige System der Fragebildung für *is/am/are* bleibt auch für die Vergangenheit gültig. Die englische Sprache entspricht hier vollständig der deutschen, folgen Sie also ruhig Ihrem Sprachgefühl.

Was it great?	War es großartig/prima?
Was the weather good?	War das Wetter gut?
Were you in Germany?	Waren Sie / Wart ihr / Warst Du in Deutschland?
Where **were** you on Monday evening?	Wo waren Sie / wart ihr / warst Du am Montag abend?
What **was** it like?	Wie war das/es?

1 Please complete the dialogue: was, wasn't, were, weren't.

A: Where ..... you yesterday evening? You weren't at the disco.
B: No, I ..... . I was at home in bed. I ..... very well. What ..... it like at the disco? ..... Jane with you?
A: Yes, she ..... . But it ..... an awful evening.
B: Why ..... that?
A: The music ..... very good. We ..... very tired, too, so we ..... home at 11.00.
B: ..... David and Iris there?
A: No, they ..... .

2 Ask questions with where/who/what/when/why.

1 ..... was with you?
2 ..... were David and Iris? They weren't at the disco.
3 ..... was Jane so tired?
4 ..... were you at the disco? Was it last Saturday?
5 ..... was the music like?

3 Where were you?

Write five sentences and say where you were.

Example:
I was at home yesterday afternoon.

Where were you:
1 last Friday at 5 pm?
2 at the weekend?
3 yesterday morning?
4 last summer?
5 last night at 2 am?

Lerntip

Sie werden vielleicht schon festgestellt haben, daß Sie weit mehr Englisch verstehen, als Sie selbst sagen können. Das ist normal – es gilt auch für Ihre Muttersprache – und auch gut so. Aktivieren Sie Ihr Englisch, das Sie verstehen, aber noch nicht sprechen, indem Sie regelmäßig in den Unterricht kommen und engagiert mitmachen, auch in der Partner- und Kleingruppenarbeit. Denn Sprechen lernen Sie nur durch Sprechen.

1 Please complete the dialogue: was or were?

A: Where ..... you on Monday evening?
B: I ..... at home all evening.
A: Well, I don't understand that,
I ..... there in the evening but you ..... not at home.
B: What time ..... you here.
A: It ..... 11 o'clock.
B: At 11 o'clock? I ..... in bed.

2 Please match.

1 What was it like?

2 How much were the bananas?

3 Were you late?

4 Why was she in bed?

5 What time was the train?

☐ a No, I was early.

☐ b She wasn't very well.

☐ c It was very exciting.

☐ d It was at 9 pm.

☐ e They were £1.50

3 Please complete Vanessa's story.

Yesterday I was in Cambridge with Sven.
It was a very exciting ..... . In the morning we were in the centre of Cambridge and then we had a ..... in a nice ..... near the river Cam.
The ..... was fine, so in the ..... we were on the ..... in a punt, that's a kind of ..... .
It was Sven's ..... time in a punt.
..... I don't know how, Sven was in the .....
We were home very late and Mum wasn't very happy!

4 Say it in English.

A: Fragen Sie, wie der Tag war.
What ....

B: Sagen Sie, daß er nicht sehr schön war.
....

A: Fragen Sie, wieso.
....

B: Sagen Sie, daß es Ihnen nicht gut ging.
I ....

A: Fragen Sie, wie es B jetzt geht.
How ....

B: Sagen Sie, daß es Ihnen gut geht.
....

STEP 2

Last year in Canada

TEXT

4 Water Tower Road
Wimbourne
Dorset
BH27 3QT

4th July

Dear John,

Thank you for your letter. You asked about our summer holiday in Canada. We were there for four weeks. We stayed with my sister and her family in Toronto for one week and then we hired a car. We visited a lot of interesting places. We stayed at a hotel in Montreal for three days and then we visited Niagara Falls. We camped near Lake Huron but it rained a lot. Then we travelled to Quebec. We arrived there at 3 o'clock in the morning and were very tired. We enjoyed our holiday in Canada very much.

What did you do in the summer? Were you in Scotland? You usually go there. Where did you stay? What was the weather like? Did it rain there too?

Love,

David and Catherine

Montreal

Niagara Falls

Quebec

ACTIVITIES

1 Comprehension

Look at the letter and answer the questions.

1 Did David and Catherine stay in Canada for four weeks? – Yes, they did.
2 Did they stay with David's brother? – No, they didn't.
3 Did they hire a car?
4 Did they visit Niagara Falls?
5 Did they stay at a hotel near Lake Huron?
6 Did they travel to Quebec?
7 Did they arrive in Quebec at four o'clock in the afternoon?
8 Did they enjoy their holiday in Canada?

2 Ask your teacher.

What did your teacher do yesterday?
Example:
Did you get up early?
Did you go to a restaurant?

Here are eight ideas.

enjoy visit start write
come read go speak

3 Ask your partner about yesterday.

Examples:
Did you travel by car?
Did you eat toast for breakfast?
Did you stay at home?

4 The class tells a story.

The story starts: At the weekend we ...

A: At the weekend we travelled by car to Austria.
B: At the weekend we travelled by car to Austria and we camped near a lake.
C: At the weekend we travelled by car to Austria and we camped near a lake ...

stay hire play visit
camp travel arrive like work
start enjoy ask rain

5 Ask your partner about a holiday.

Use the words in Exercise 4. Example:
Where were you on holiday?
Where did you stay?
Did you enjoy it?
What was the weather like?

Listening & pronunciation

6a Listen and repeat.

[d]	[t]	[ɪd]
travell**ed**	camp**ed**	start**ed**
arriv**ed**	ask**ed**	visit**ed**
enjoy**ed**	work**ed**	
stay**ed**	lik**ed**	

I arriv**ed** on Saturday.
I lik**ed** the hotel.
I visit**ed** the museum.

6b Listen and answer.

Paul tells a friend about his holiday in Canada. Look at the two maps and listen. What is right: map A or map B?

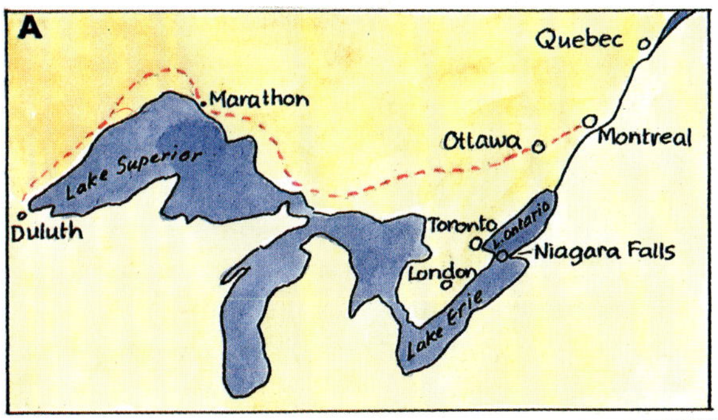

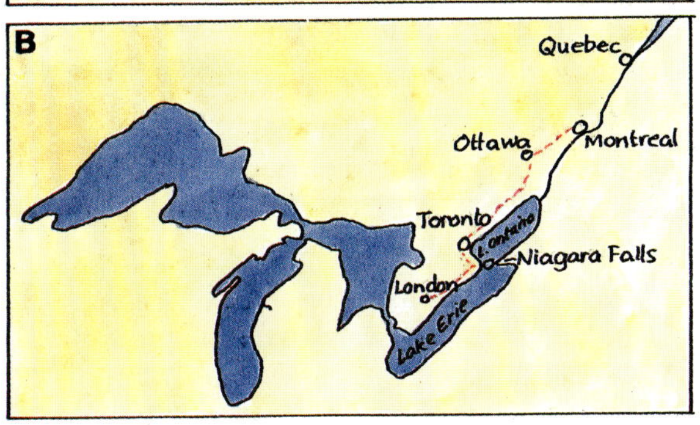

GRAMMAR

1 Die Vergangenheitsform mit *-ed:*

Die einfache Vergangenheit der sogenannten 'regelmäßigen' Verben setzt sich zusammen aus ihrer Grundform und der Endung *-ed*. Diese Endung wird unterschiedlich ausgesprochen, je nachdem welcher Laut ihr vorausgeht.

He stay**ed** at a hotel.	[d] nach stimmhaftem Laut
We camp**ed** in Canada.	[t] nach stimmlosem Laut
They visit**ed** Edinburgh.	[ɪd] nach [t] und [d]

2 Fragen und Kurzantworten in der Vergangenheit mit *did:*

Sie stellen Fragen über die Vergangenheit, indem Sie für alle Personen (auch für *he, she, it*) *did* benutzen.
In den Kurzantworten wird diese Form *did* wieder aufgenommen.

Frage	Kurzantwort
Did you visit Paris?	Yes, I **did**. No, I **didn't**.
Did he travel by train?	Yes, he **did**. No, he **didn't**.
Did you enjoy your holiday?	Yes, we **did**. No, we **didn't**.
Did they hire a car?	Yes, they **did**. No, they **didn't**.

3 Zeitangaben mit *yesterday, last week, last summer* usw:

In Aussagen und Fragesätzen der Vergangenheit finden sich häufig Zeitangaben wie *yesterday, last week*. In Fragesätzen befinden sich diese Zeitangaben am Satzende. In Aussagesätzen stehen sie entweder am Satzanfang oder -ende.

What did you do **yesterday**?
Where did you stay in Scotland **last summer**?

Yesterday	I hired a boat.
	I hired a boat **yesterday**.
Last summer	it rained a lot.
	It rained a lot **last summer.**

Tip: Stellen Sie Ihre Zeitangaben an den Anfang Ihrer Aussagesätze. Sie werden dann an die richtige zu verwendende Zeitform des Verbs erinnert.

1 Please complete.

Complete with: did/(hire)/(camp)/(rain)/(stay).

(D = David, J = John)
D: Where ..... you stay in Scotland last summer?
J: I ..... in Inverness.
D: ..... you camp or stay at a hotel?
J: I ..... near the lake. I don't like hotels.
D: ..... it rain a lot? It often rains in August.
J: Well, it ..... the first week, but then the weather was very good.
D: ..... you hire a boat?
J: Yes, I ..... a boat the second week. I enjoyed the holiday very much. I love Scotland.

2 Look and answer.

Look at exercise 1. Answer the questions with: Yes, ... did or No, ... didn't.

1 Did John go to Scotland?
2 Did he stay in Edinburgh?
3 Did he camp near a lake?
4 Did it rain a lot in the first week?
5 Did he hire a car?
6 Did he enjoy the holiday?

3 And now you.

Write a postcard or letter to a friend about your last summer holiday. Here are nine ideas:

stay	rain	arrive
play	camp	...
hire	travel	...
visit	enjoy	...

Start the letter/postcard like this:
Dear ...

HOMESTUDY

Lerntip

Auswendiglernen kann lästig werden, wenn Sie versuchen, wahllos alles Wichtige und Unwichtige durcheinander zu memorieren. Wenn Sie aber zunächst entscheiden, welche Wörter, Wendungen und Sätze Ihnen wichtig und notwendig sind und diese gezielt lernen, werden Sie feststellen, daß das Auswendiglernen effektiv Nutzen bringt und sogar Freude machen kann. Wählen Sie z.B. ein paar Wörter aus einem bestimmten Wortfeld aus und prägen Sie sich diese ein. Oder suchen Sie sich Teile der Dialoge aus, die Sie als nützliche Redewendungen in einem natürlichen Zusammenhang auswendiglernen können.

1 Picture story

Please complete the text with: (rain)/(camp)/(enjoy)/(play)/(travel)/(visit)/(arrive)/(hire)

Last summer Peter and Susan were in the Lake District. They ..... a car and ..... to the Lake District. They ..... at Lake Windermere at 2 pm. They ..... next to the lake. In the afternoon they ..... tennis. On Sunday it ..... all day. In the afternoon they ..... a folk museum. It was very interesting and they ..... it there very much.

2 Match and write the sentences.

Look at the letter on page 84 again.

We	hired	with my sister in Toronto
We	stayed	to Quebec
We	visited	near Lake Huron
We	travelled	a car
We	camped	Niagara Falls

3 What is the right order?

A's questions are right, but B's answers are in the wrong order.

A: When did you start your first job?
B: *Oh, yes I did, very much.*
A: Where did you work?
B: *I opened it in 1989. I'm very happy now. It's great.*
A: Did you like it there?
B: *I opened a restaurant.*
A: So, why did you leave?
B: *I started my first job in 1985.*
A: And when did you open your restaurant?
B: *In a German restaurant in London.*

4 Say it in English.

Sie schreiben eine Postkarte/einen Brief. Sie:

1 beginnen mit der Anrede:
2 bedanken sich für den Brief Ihres Briefpartners / Ihrer Briefpartnerin.
3 fragen, wie es ihm/ihr geht.
4 fragen ihn/sie, ob ihm/ihr der Urlaub gefallen hat.
5 schließen mit einem Gruß.

☐ a How are you?
☐ b Love, ...
☐ c Did you enjoy your holiday
☐ d Dear ...
☐ e Thank you for your letter.

STEP 3

London is great!

STARTER

1 Revision: Memory game

Look at page 84 for one minute.

Now close your books. What can you remember about David and Catherine's holiday in Canada?

2 Vocabulary

Match the verbs: come, go, see.
Yesterday we **went** on a tour of London. We **saw** a lot of interesting places. We **came** home at 10 pm.

DIALOGUE

Part 1

(C = Chris, T = Tina, M = Mark)

C: So, what time did you come home yesterday?
T: Oh, we came home very late. We were in London all day.
C: Great! Where did you go?
M: We went to the London Transport Museum and stayed there all morning. It was so interesting.
T: Yes, we saw everything.
M: Then we went to the London Docklands and had lunch in a lovely restaurant. In the afternoon we went on a tour of London. We saw Buckingham Palace and the Tower of London and the Houses of Parliament, oh and then we went to ...

Part 2

M: ... oh yes, and then we went to Trafalgar Square and Piccadilly Circus.
C: Really? So, did you enjoy the tour?
M: Yes, I did. It was great.
T: Well, I didn't like it very much. Docklands was interesting but the tour of London was too long. We travelled around by bus for four hours!
C: So you saw everything ...
T: No, not everything. We didn't see the Queen. She's on holiday in Scotland ...

ACTIVITIES

Part 1

1a Talk about Tina and Mark's day.

Example:
They came home very late.
They ...

visited came had saw went

1b Ask your teacher.

You'd like to ask your teacher about a place he/she visited (in 19..). First write down 5-7 questions. Then ask your teacher.

Examples: Where did you go (in 19..)?
What did you visit there?
Did you enjoy it?

Here are eight ideas: have? see? visit? go? travel? play? arrive? rain?

1c Ask your partner.

Now ask your partner about a place he or she visited in ... . Write down the answers and then tell your teacher / the class.

Example: Brigitte went to Strasbourg last weekend / in 1990 / on Saturday. She visited...

Part 2

2a What is wrong with the story?

Read the dialogue on page 88 again.
Now read this. What is wrong?

Tina and Vanessa went to London yesterday. They went to the London Transport Museum and stayed there all day. Then they went to Oxford Street and had lunch in an awful cafe. They went on a tour of London in the evening and saw the Queen. They travelled by bus for six hours.

Example:
Vanessa didn't go to London.
Mark went to London.

2b When I was fourteen ...

This is what Vanessa's life is like:

Vanessa has got a mountain bike and a skateboard. She sometimes goes on holiday with her friends and not with her mother and father. She sometimes stays at her friend's house at the weekend. She goes to school by bus. She plays tennis at school. She usually goes to bed at 10.00 pm. On Saturday she sometimes goes to a disco with her friends and comes home at 11.00. She goes to bed at 11.30. She has parties at home with her friends.

What was your life like when you were fourteen?

Example: When I was fourteen I didn't have a mountain bike.

Listening & pronunciation

3a Listen again.

Listen to the dialogue parts 1-2 again.

3b Listen and repeat.

Will man im Satz eine bestimmte Information hervorheben, betont man das betreffende Wort stärker. Hören Sie die Sätze und unterstreichen Sie das Wort, das betont wird. Beim zweiten Mal sprechen Sie die Sätze nach.

1 Well, we saw everything.
2 No, I didn't, I came home early.
3 Her hat is awful.
4 No, she works for a Swedish radio station.
5 I went there with Vanessa.
6 No, turn right into Bridge Street.
7 But that's their winter.

3c Listen and answer.

Listen to the information about a tour of London and answer the questions.

1 When does the tour leave?
2 Where does it start?
3 How long is the tour?
4 How much is it? (→ *Andere Länder, andere Sitten*)

GRAMMAR

1 Unregelmäßige Verben und ihre Vergangenheitsformen:

Unregelmäßige Verben sind solche, die ihre Vergangenheitsform nicht mit *-ed* bilden, sondern eine eigene Form haben. Diese müssen Sie lernen. Doch nur keine Angst! Sie werden sie so oft benutzen, daß Ihnen diese Formen sehr bald geläufig werden. Häufig gebrauchte unregelmäßige Verben sind z.B.:

Gegenwart	I come	I do	I go	I have	I see
Vergangenheit	I **came**	I **did**	I **went**	I **had**	I **saw**

Jetzt haben Sie einige wichtige Vergangenheitsformen kennengelernt – denken Sie nur einmal daran, daß eigentlich auch *was* und *were* in diese Aufzählung gehören –, die Sie benötigen, um Unterhaltungen wie die folgende zu führen:

– What time did you come home yesterday?
– I came home very late. I was in London all day.
– Where did you go?
– I went to the London Docklands. It was great.

2 Verneinung in der Vergangenheit mit *didn't*:

Die Verneinung regelmäßiger und unregelmäßiger Verben verläuft nach bekanntem Muster. Hängen Sie einfach *n't* an *did* oder stellen Sie *not* nach und benutzen Sie danach das Vollverb in seiner Grundform.

We **saw** Buckingham Palace,
but we **didn't / did not see** the Queen.

We **liked** the tour,
but we **didn't / did not like** the weather.

Das Verb *be* bleibt sich selbst treu und nimmt auch hier eine Sonderstellung ein:

I **was** at the office,
but Peter **wasn't / was not** there.

We **were** very tired,
but you **weren't / were not**.

1 Please complete.

(M = Mother, D = Daughter)

M: Where did you (go) yesterday evening?
D: I (go) to the cinema.
M: What did you (see) there?
D: I (see) Dustin Hoffman in Rain Man.
M: Did you (like) it?
D: Yes, I (like) it very much. Dustin Hoffman was great.
M: Who did you (go) with?
D: I (go) with Peter and Rosalind.
M: Did you (have) a nice time?
D: Yes, we (have) a lovely time.

2 Please complete with a negative.

1 She had a cup of coffee but she didn't have lunch.
2 You saw a lot in the museum but ..... everything.
3 They went to Canada for their holidays but they ..... Quebec.
4 We came home very early but we ..... by car.
5 I liked London but I ..... the bus tour.

3 What was your weekend like?

Write three positive and three negative sentences about your weekend.

see a film
visit a friend
go to a museum
go to a restaurant
stay at home
come home late

HOMESTUDY

Lerntip

In diesem Kurs sind die Grammatikerklärungen kein Selbstzweck, sie sind vielmehr als praktische Orientierungshilfe gedacht und deswegen mit handfesten Übungen eng verzahnt. Sie lernen die neue Grammatik zunächst im Zusammenhang, dann erst als Regel. Es ist nützlich, die Grammatikseiten aus den vorangegangenen Lektionen nach einer Weile noch einmal durchzuarbeiten. Dadurch verhindern Sie, daß Wichtiges in Vergessenheit gerät.

1 Reading

This is Joanne's diary. Read about her week. Do you understand it?

MONDAY 4TH JULY
I arrived late for work. Mr Jones wasn't very happy so I didn't have lunch but worked in the office.

TUESDAY 5TH JULY
I went with my mother to visit her sister. We stayed all evening. I didn't really enjoy it. Tim wasn't there.

WEDNESDAY 6TH JULY
I had lunch with Nicola in a lovely restaurant near the office.

THURSDAY 7TH JULY
I played tennis at the club at 6 o'clock. Then we went to a café for a drink.

FRIDAY 8TH JULY
I wasn't well so I stayed at home, but I was OK in the evening.

SATURDAY 9TH JULY
Nicola came. She stayed for 2 hours then we went to the cinema. We saw Batman. It wasn't very good.

SUNDAY 10TH JULY
The weather was awful. It rained all day. I was tired so I stayed at home. In the evening I saw a film on TV.

2 Now answer the questions.

1 When did Joanne have lunch with Nicola? She had lunch ...
2 Where did they have lunch? They ...
3 Did Joanne have lunch on Monday? What did she do?
4 What was the weather like on Sunday?
5 Why did Joanne stay at home on Sunday?
6 Who did Joanne go to the cinema with on Saturday?
7 What did they see?
8 Where did Joanne go with her mother?
9 Why didn't she enjoy it?
10 Why didn't she go to work on Friday?

3 A wordpuzzle

Find the ten past tenses.

S	A	W	T	A	B	L	E	P	A
T	R	A	D	E	H	W	J	L	E
R	O	S	C	A	M	E	L	A	D
A	N	O	P	E	T	N	Y	Y	S
V	A	P	S	O	N	T	K	E	T
E	R	E	N	J	O	Y	E	D	A
L	O	N	D	O	N	A	D	A	R
L	A	E	T	H	A	D	F	U	T
E	L	D	E	R	A	B	B	I	E
D	E	A	R	O	H	I	R	E	D

4 Say it in English.

Sie möchten jemanden fragen, ob:

1 er/sie Mittag in einem Pub gegessen hat.
– Did you ...?
2 ihm/ihr die Stadtrundfahrt gefallen hat.
– Did you ...?
3 er/sie alles gesehen hat.
– Did you ...?
4 er/sie den ganzen Tag dort geblieben ist.
– Did you ...?
5 er/sie spät nach Hause gekommen ist.
– Did you ...?

REVISION AND EXTENSION

• Starter

1 Where were they? ...
2 What did they do? ...
3 What was the weather like? ...

Our day in Cambridge

1 Find the opposites.

Find the opposites and write them down.

morning	–	winter
last week	–	late
come	–	evening
lovely	–	day
early	–	never
arrive	–	go
night	–	next week
summer	–	awful
always	–	leave

morning – evening
last week – ...
come – ...
...

2 What's the right order?

1 Scotland / summer / travelled / we / to / Last.
2 went / train / there / We / by.
3 very / exciting / Edinburgh / was.
4 interesting / of / saw / a / We / streets / lot.
5 often / didn't / It / very / rain / in Scotland.
6 car / two / for / hired / a / We / days.
7 lovely / was / summer holiday / a / It.

3 Your class list

What they did:	Names		
had a nice breakfast	Gill ✔	Bob ✗	Bill ✔
enjoyed the day			
had lunch with friends			
went to the cinema			

(✔= Yes, I did.) (✗ = No, I didn't.)

Look at the class list. Write the questions with *did*:

Did you have a nice breakfast yesterday?
Did ...

Now ask 3 students what they did yesterday. Write their names in the list – with ✔ or ✗.

Then tell your class like this: Gill and Bill had a nice breakfast yesterday but Bob didn't (have a nice breakfast).

4 Summer or winter?

What did you sometimes/often/never do last summer. Write 3 things.

And what did you sometimes/often/never do last winter. Write 3 things.

Then tell your partner.

went to a museum
went to bed early
played tennis
had a lot of ice-cream
played Monopoly

REVISION AND EXTENSION

5 And now you.

Tell your neighbour what you did last Saturday or last Sunday. Start like this:

Last Saturday (Sunday) I ...

Say what you did in the morning, in the afternoon and in the evening.

6 Sweet Sixteen.

Can you remember what you did when you were 16? Work in groups of 4 or 5 and talk to the students in your group. Ask questions and answer.

Where did you live?
Did you live at home?
Did you have a lot of friends?
Did you go to discos/parties?
What did you do in the evening?
Did you have a boyfriend/girlfriend?...
Did you go to bed early/late?
How did you go to school?
Did you drink beer?

7 Memory check

What words from Unit 5 can you remember? Write them down. What were your neighbour's words?

8 Reading

King's Lynn is an interesting old town on the river Ouse. It's got a lot of beautiful old houses and two market places – the Tuesday Market Place and the Saturday Market Place.

It has also got a modern shopping centre, the Vancouver Centre. The name comes from George Vancouver, one of King's Lynn's famous citizens. He founded the city of Vancouver in Canada.

The town has also got two museums, two cinemas, a sports centre, a football club and a golf club. There are lovely parks and gardens, and in the summer there is a festival. Why not go and see it?

Option:
Write about your town or city or about a place that you like. Ask your teacher for help.

• Useful phrases

Goodbye

Boats by the sea

The beach at Hunstanton

A Norfolk village

A Norfolk windmill

Unit 6

Helen erzählt etwas aus ihrem Leben und während eines Strandpicknicks berichten Tina und Mark, was sie im Urlaub erlebt haben. Sie verabschieden sich und tauschen Adressen aus.
In dieser Unit lernen Sie u.a.:

- etwas über den eigenen Lebensweg erzählen
- Urlaubserlebnisse berichten und erfragen
- Namen und Adressen buchstabieren
- sich bedanken und verabschieden.

STEP 1

A life history

STARTER

Vocabulary

Look at the pictures. They are about Karel, the Czech guest at the bed-and-breakfast in Unit 5. Match the sentences and the pictures.

1 He was born in a Prague hospital.
2 He met Martina, his wife, at a cinema.
3 He got married when he was 30.
4 He started his business in 1990.

a

b

c

d

DIALOGUE

(R = Reporter, H = Helen)

R: When did you start your business?
H: We started the bed-and-breakfast thirteen years ago.
R: And why did you start a bed-and-breakfast business?
H: Well, we had a big house and we didn't have very much money. My husband didn't have a job at the time and I didn't work full-time.
R: Why not?
H: I was at home, you see. Vanessa was very small. She was born when John was ten.
R: Where did you meet your husband?
H: Oh, I met Norman in a London hospital. I trained there from 1968 to 1971. We got married in 1970.
R: Do you like your work at the B & B?
H: Yes, I do. We meet a lot of interesting people from different countries and they often write to us.
R: Do you sometimes visit them?
H: No, we don't.
R: Oh, why not?
H: Well, we've got the money now, but we haven't got the time.
(→ *Andere Länder, andere Sitten*)

ACTIVITIES

1 Comprehension

Listen to the dialogue and answer the questions.

1 Did Helen's husband, Norman, have a job when they started the business?
2 Did they have a small house?
3 How old was John when Vanessa was born?
4 Where did Helen train?
5 When did they get married?
6 Does Helen like her work?
7 How often do they visit their guests?

2 What year is it?

1 1929 2 1066 3 1934 4 1492 5 1688 6 1945

3 Ask your partner.

Example:
A: What (day) was it (two days) ago?
B: It was (Wednesday).
A: What (year) was it (three years) ago?
B: It was nineteen ...

4 Ask your partner: When did you ...?

When did you	have your first television?
	have your first car?
	have your first telephone?
	have your first bike?
	come to your first English class?
	go on your first holiday?
	start your first job?

Use these words in your answers:

I had / came to / went on / started my first ...		
last year	3 hours ago	when I was 10
last week	2 days ago	when I was 20
last Monday	5 weeks ago	in 1975
last summer	10 years ago	in 1982
last winter		

Example:
A: When did you have your first car?
B: I haven't got a car. / I had my first car 13 years ago.

Now tell your class about your partner.

5 Ask your teacher ...

1 ... where she/he was born
2 ... where she/he went to school
3 ... how long he/she trained
4 ... what her /his first job was

Example: Where were you born?

Now ask your partner questions and fill in the form.

Name:	
Born in (place):	
Started school:	
Went to school in:	
Trained:	
First worked:	
Then worked:	
Got married:	
Son/Daughter was born:	

Listening & pronunciation

6a Listen and repeat: [ə]

We started th**e** bed-**a**nd-breakf**a**st thirteen years **a**go.
My husb**a**nd didn't have **a** job **a**t th**e** time.
I was **a**t home.
V**a**ness**a** w**a**s born when John w**a**s ten.
Hel**e**n met Norm**a**n in Lond**o**n.
We hav**e**n't got th**e** time.
V**a**ness**a** is Helen's daught**er**.

6b Listen and answer.

The reporter talks to Karel about the bed-and-breakfast. Listen to the dialogue, listen again, then complete the reporter's notes.

Where's the guest from?	*Prague*
What does he think of the B&B?	*He says ...*
Does he often come here?	*...*

GRAMMAR

1 Unregelmäßige Verben und ihre Vergangenheitsform:

In Unit 5 Step 3 lernten Sie die Vergangenheitsformen einiger wichtiger unregelmäßiger Verben. Hier finden Sie eine um die neuen Formen aus Unit 6 Step 1 erweiterte Liste.

am/is	–	**was**	go	–	**went**
are	–	**were**	have	–	**had**
come	–	**came**	meet	–	**met**
do	–	**did**	see	–	**saw**
get	–	**got**			

2 Zeitangaben der Vergangenheit:

When I was 20 I met my husband.
Als ich 20 war, ...
Ten years ago we got married.
Vor 10 Jahren ...
In 1985 our son Peter was born.
Im Jahre 1985 ...
Last year we met the Brown family.
Im letzten Jahr/Letztes Jahr ...

Ten years ago = Vor zehn Jahren

3 Wie Sie nach dem Alter fragen:

How old are you?	Wie alt bist Du / sind Sie?
When were you born?	Wann wurdest Du / wurden Sie geboren?
How old is he/she?	Wie alt ist er/sie?
When was he/she born?	Wann wurde er/sie geboren?

1 Please complete.

Complete Mark's questions with *did*, then look at the dialogue again. Fill in the right form of the verbs in Chris' answers: meet, play, open, come, have.

M: When ..... you come to King's Lynn?
C: I ..... two years ago. Procomp, my firm ..... a new office here.
M: ..... you ask to come?
C: Yes, I did.
M: Where ..... you meet John?
C: We ..... at the sports centre in King's Lynn.
M: When was that?
C: Last year. On Thursday evenings we ..... squash and one evening we ..... a drink in the bar. We're great friends now.

2 What is right?

A: Do/Did/Does you go to see David at the hospital yesterday?
B: Yes, I see/saw/sees David for an hour in the afternoon.
A: I don't/doesn't/aren't visit him very often because I work/worked/works full-time.
B: Does/Did/Do a lot of people visit him?
A: Yes, he gets/has got/got a lot of friends and they come to see him. Yesterday I meet/meets/met his sister for the first time. She's very nice.

3 And now you.

Write ten sentences about your life and work or about a member of your family or a friend.

Example:
I was born in Landshut. I started school in 19... and I started work in 19..

HOMESTUDY

Lerntip

Auch Lesen ist eine Fertigkeit, die man lernen muß. Auf dieser Homestudy-Seite finden Sie eine Leseverständnisübung mit einem Text, der z.T. unbekannte Wörter enthält. Lassen Sie sich dadurch nicht irritieren und greifen Sie bitte nicht gleich zum Wörterbuch. Lesen Sie den Text kurz durch, um einen Eindruck davon zu bekommen, wovon er in etwa handelt. Lesen Sie dann die Fragen: sie helfen Ihnen, sich ein genaueres Bild vom Inhalt zu machen. Bei Ihrer zweiten Lektüre versuchen Sie festzustellen, in welchen Zeilen des Textes die Antworten auf die Fragen zu finden sind. Markieren Sie sie. Danach erst beantworten Sie die Fragen soweit wie möglich. Lesen Sie den Text ein letztes Mal: jetzt werden Sie hoffentlich feststellen, daß Sie das meiste verstanden haben – ohne im Wörterbuch nachzuschlagen. Die Wörter, die Sie noch nicht entschlüsselt haben, können also doch nicht so wichtig gewesen sein.

1 Reading

A BOOMING BED-AND-BREAKFAST BUSINESS. PROFILE ON HELEN KEMP.

This week our reporter Jonathan Williams interviewed Mrs Helen Kemp, who has a bed-and-breakfast in King's Lynn.

Helen, a very active and attractive lady, has a teen-age daughter, Vanessa, and a son, John, who works in a bank. Helen says that she has a lot to do in the bed-and-breakfast, but she enjoys her work because she meets a lot of interesting people from different countries. Guests from all over Europe, Germany, Sweden, Italy and Switzerland stay at the B&B. "They often come again," Helen says with a smile. Helen started the business 13 years ago when Vanessa was only 2 and her husband, Norman, didn't have a job. "We wanted to start a new life. It was awful at first but now we are very happy." Helen's husband Norman works for a garage in King's Lynn now. He's a car mechanic. "My family are great," says Helen. "They help me a lot in the B&B at the weekends, and we love the life here." Good luck to Helen Kemp and all her family!

2 Please answer the questions.

1 Why does Helen enjoy her work?
2 Where do her guests come from?
3 Did Norman have a job when they started the B&B?
4 When did Helen start the business?
5 How old was Vanessa when Helen started the business?
6 What was it like when Helen first started the business?
7 Where does Norman work now?

3 Please put the words into three groups.

Work	Sport	Holiday
business	*game*	*B&B*
...	...	...

travel
squash
business
play
full-time
postcard
job
firm
ice-hockey
camp
B&B
game

4 Say it in English.

Sie möchten Norman fragen:

1 wann er geboren ist	When ... born?
2 wann er geheiratet hat	When ... married?
3 wann er seine Frau kennengelernt hat	When ... wife?
4 wann seine Tochter geboren ist	When ... born?

STEP 2

A beach picnic

STARTER

1 Revision

Work in groups of four. Write down four words from Step 1. Give the words to another group. They make four sentences or questions with your words. Read the sentences to the class.

2 Vocabulary

Look at the photos on page 94-95. Ask your partner questions. Example:

A: What do you think of (Hunstanton)?
B: I like it / I don't like it.

I think I don't think	it's	(too) ... (very) ...

quiet	exciting	lovely
crowded	big	great
relaxing	small	awful
interesting	nice	

Use the words in the box. Do you understand them? Ask your teacher for help.

DIALOGUE

(V = Vanessa, H = Helen, N = Norman, M = Mark, C = Chris, A = Astrid, K = Karel)

V: Can you pass me the sandwiches?
H: Here you are.
V: Oh, and I'd like the ketchup, too.
H: Have you got everything now, Vanessa?
V: Yes, thanks.
N: So, this is your last day, Mark. Did you enjoy your holiday in Norfolk?
M: Yes, I did. I like Norfolk very much. The villages are lovely. Tina and I had tea yesterday in Burnham Market, a nice village near here.
N: Did you buy souvenirs to take home?
M: Well, Tina bought me a black umbrella.
N: And what did you buy her?
M: A tea cosy.
C: That's very English!
N: And what do you think of Norfolk, Astrid?
A: Oh, I think it's quiet and relaxing but I didn't really like Hunstanton. It was too crowded when we were there last Sunday.
K: Can I take a photo of you all?
H: That's a nice idea. Can you send us one for our photo album?
K: Of course. Come on – smile.

ACTIVITIES

1 Comprehension

Listen to the dialogue and answer the questions.

1 What would Vanessa like with her sandwiches?
2 Is it Mark's first day in King's Lynn?
3 What does Mark think of the villages?
4 What did Tina buy Mark? (use: *him*)
5 What did Mark buy Tina? (use: *her*)
6 Why didn't Astrid like Hunstanton?
7 Does Vanessa take the photo?
8 Why would Helen like a photo, too?

2 Roleplay: At a picnic.

apples sandwiches
hamburgers ketchup bananas
biscuits water coke

You are at a picnic. Ask your partner for food.

Example:
A: Can you pass me (a hamburger), please.
B: Here you are.
A: Thanks. And I'd like the ketchup, too, please.
B: Here you are.

3 What presents did you buy?

You were in London yesterday. You bought presents for: Mr and Mrs Wilson, Helen and Norman, Vanessa, Tina and Mark, John, Chris, Astrid. What presents did you buy? Please fill in the table. Here are seven ideas for presents: tea cosy, umbrella, dictionary, cup, biscuits, photo of the Queen, map.

Mr & Mrs Wilson	
Helen & Norman	
Vanessa	
Tina & Mark	
John	
Chris	
Astrid	

Now ask your partner what he/she bought.

Example: A: What did you buy Tina and Mark?
B: I bought them an umbrella.

4 Roleplay

Complete these sentences and match them to the pictures:
1 ..... take your photo, please?
2 ..... camp here, please?
3 ..... help you?

Now choose one picture. You and your partner are the people in the picture. Have a conversation.

Listening & pronunciation

5a Listen and repeat.

In some words the letter "s" is [s] and in others it is [z]. How do you say "please"? How do you say "thanks". What about "souvenirs"?
Now listen and repeat.

thanks –	please	smile	– museum
this –	tea cosy	it's	– he's
last –	hairdryers	yesterday	– villages
send –	pubs		

When does the post office close?
Sven would like to send six postcards to his Swedish friends.
He's got souvenirs for his sons.

5b Listen and answer.

In the shop:

1 She'd like a cat.	2 It's £22.
She'd like a hat.	It's £2.
She'd like a big hat.	It's £20.

GRAMMAR

1 Wie Sie jemanden um etwas bitten:

Can I take a photo ...?	Kann/Darf ich ein Photo ... machen?
Can you send us one?	Kannst Du / Können Sie uns eines schicken?

2 Fragesätze mit *can* und *have got*:

Aussage	Frage
You **can** camp here.	**Can** I camp here?
I **have got** everything.	**Have** you **got** everything?

Diese Fragen werden wie im Deutschen gebildet. Übrigens gilt das auch für Fragesätze, die mit einem Fragewort beginnen:

What can I do for you?
Where can I see you?

3 Wie Sie ausdrücken, daß Sie etwas haben möchten:

I'd like the ketchup.	Ich möchte gern den Ketchup (haben).
We'd like the umbrella.	Wir möchten gern den Schirm (haben).

Diese Wendung haben Sie bereits einmal in Unit 4 kennengelernt. Bitte verwechseln Sie nicht *I'd like* mit *I like*, das "Ich mag/Ich habe gern ..." bedeutet.

4 Die persönlichen Fürwörter *me, you, him, her, us, them*:

me	mich	Peter and Jill visited me yesterday.
you	dich/Sie/euch	They saw you on Monday.
him	ihn	You didn't see him.
her	sie	Did you see her?
it	es	What's their phone number? Have you got it?
us	uns	They like us.
them	sie	Do you like them?

1 Please complete.

(V = Vanessa, H = Helen, T = Tina)

1 me/him/her/them.

V: I saw Peter yesterday.
H: Where did you see ......
V: In the supermarket. He was with a lady but I didn't know ......
H: Did you speak to .....?
V: No, they didn't see ..... .

2 her/us/me

T: I'd like a photo with Mark. Can you take one of ....., please, Vanessa.
V: Oh, yes I can, but can you take one of ....., too.
T: Of course. Mark can you pass ..... the camera, so she can take a photo of ..... .

2 Please complete: like / 'd like.

(T = Tina, M = Mark, A = Assistant)

T: Would you really ..... an umbrella, Mark?
M: Yes, I ..... a nice English one. And what would you ..... – a tea cosy?!
T: Why not?
M: OK, you buy me an umbrella and I can buy you a tea cosy.
T: We ..... this umbrella, please.
A: Is that all, Madam?
T: No, I ..... a tea cosy please.
A: I'm sorry Madam. We haven't got tea cosies. They've got tea cosies in the shop opposite.
T: Here's your umbrella, Mark. Do you ..... it?
M: Yes, thanks. I ..... it a lot.

HOMESTUDY

Lerntip

Überlegen Sie einmal, wo Ihre Stärken und Schwächen beim Englischlernen liegen. Beim Sprechen? Lesen? Hörverstehen? Wortschatzlernen? Bei der Aussprache oder Grammatik? Sie haben doch bestimmt ein sicheres Gefühl dafür, was Ihnen leichter und was Ihnen schwerer fällt. Achten Sie darauf, daß Sie auch die Bereiche trainieren, die Ihnen nicht so liegen und u.U. nicht so viel Spaß machen. Nutzen Sie die Übungsmöglichkeiten im Unterricht und auch zuhause. Lesen Sie, wenn es Ihnen hilft, nochmal die Lerntips dieses Buches durch. Und bitten Sie Ihren Kursleiter / Ihre Kursleiterin ggf. um Rat. Scheuen Sie sich nicht, denn kaum jemand ist beim Sprachlernen in allen Bereichen gleich fit.

1 Please complete with the past tenses.

ACROSS
3 enjoys
5 is
7 hires

DOWN
1 buys
2 meets
4 has
5 goes
6 sees

2 Please complete.

(T = Tina, V = Vanessa, M = Mark, C = Chris)

1 you/us/them

V: Can I come and see ..... and Mark in Germany?
T: Of course you can come and see ..... . Write to ..... and tell ..... when you'd like to come. But ask your Mum and Dad first!
V: I asked ..... and they say it's OK.

2 us/you/it

M: Tina and I had tea in Burnham Market yesterday.
C: Did you enjoy .....?
M: Yes, it was very nice.
C: Was Vanessa with .....?
M: No, she wasn't with ..... . She was at home.

3 What does she say?

She thinks:	She says:
1 I'd like to take a photo of you.	Can I ..., please?
2 I'd like to have the ketchup.	Can I ..., please?
3 I'd like to see you again.	Can I ..., please?
4 I'd like a game of tennis.	Can we ..., please?
5 I'd like to speak to Helen.	Can I ..., please?

4 Say it in English.

Was sagen Sie, wenn Sie:

1 die Kekse wollen, die am anderen Tischende sind?	Can ...
2 auch ein Sandwich wollen?	I'd ...
3 jemandem etwas geben ?	Here ...
4 wissen wollen, was jemand von Norfolk hält?	What ...
5 ein Foto von jemandem machen wollen?	Can ...

STEP 3

Thanks for everything

STARTER

1 Revision

buy
play
pass
have
hire
take
read
send

umbrella
souvenir
sandwiches
job
postcards
stamps
car
photo
coffee
dictionary
tennis
newspaper

Ask questions like this:
Can I have a sandwich, please?
Can you pass me the newspaper, please?

2 Vocabulary

Look and listen.

A B C D E F G H I J
K L M N O P Q R S T
U V W X Y Z

Now listen and repeat.

DIALOGUE & TEXT

(N = Norman, V = Vanessa, M = Mark, T = Tina, H = Helen)

N: You must come again next year.
V: Can I have your address? I'd like to visit you in Hamburg one day.
M: It's Rotfuchsstraße 27b.
V: Can you spell that, please?
M: R-O-T-F-U-C-H-S-S-T-R-A-S-S-E 27b and it's 20005 Hamburg.
T: Come on, Mark. Our taxi's here. I'm sorry we must go now. Thanks for everything.
M: Yes, and we really enjoyed the picnic yesterday.
H: It was nice to see you again, Tina, and it was lovely to meet you, Mark.
T: Say goodbye to all the guests for us.
N: OK. Goodbye. Have a good trip.
V: Please, write.
M: Goodbye everyone. See you again next year.
All: Bye.

Dear Karen and Paul,
Thank you very much for everything.
We had a lovely time in King's Lynn.
Helen and Norman were so friendly.
We hope you had a nice time in Wales.
Love,
Tina and Mark

ACTIVITIES

1 Talk to a partner.

Speak this dialogue with a partner.

A: My name's Robyn Lowen.
B: Can you spell that, please.
A: Yes, it's R-O-B-Y-N L-O-W-E-N. And my address is 12 Knowsley Street, Throope.
B: Can you spell that, too, please.
A: It's K-N-O-W-S-L-E-Y Street in T-H-R-O-O-P-E.

And now you. Tell your partner your name and address. (→ *Andere Länder, andere Sitten*)

2 Exchange information with your partner.

A: look at this page. B: look at page 113.
A: here are two sentences. They are in code. B has got the code. Tell B the numbers. He/She says the letters. What are the two sentences?

Sentence 1:
4 22 26 15 15 19 26 23 26 15 12 5 22 15 2 7 18 14 22 19 22 9 22.

Sentence 2:
8 22 22 2 12 6 13 22 3 7 2 22 26 9.

3 Roleplay (→ *Andere Länder, andere Sitten*)

Thanks for everything.
Thanks very much for ...
We really enjoyed the ...
We had a lovely time/evening.
Say goodbye to ... for us/me.

You must come again.
It was nice to see you again.
It was lovely to meet you.
Have a nice evening.
Have a good trip.

1 You are Tina or Mark. Thank Helen or Norman and say goodbye.

2 You had a meal with a friend at his/her house. Thank him/her and say goodbye.

Now thank your teacher and say goodbye to the students in the class. Tell them your address and ask for their address.

Listening & pronunciation

4a Listen and repeat.

Achten Sie bei den Sätzen auf das Auf und Ab der Stimme. Die Höhen und Tiefen sind bei Engländern und Amerikanern stärker ausgeprägt als bei deutschen Muttersprachlern. Das klingt für deutsche Ohren oft gekünstelt. Doch versuchen Sie, die Satzmelodie nachzumachen. Sonst besteht die Gefahr, daß Sie sich für englische Ohren lustlos und gelangweilt anhören.

Hello everyone!
Nice to meet you.
Are you German?
Really? That's interesting!
I'm sorry I wasn't at your party.
Never mind.
I must go now.
Goodbye and thanks for everything.
You're welcome.
You must come and visit us.
Have a good trip.

4b Listen and answer.

Peter talks to Gillian. Listen to the dialogue, read the questions, listen again and then answer the questions. What is right?

1 Peter met Gillian for the first time
 a at a pub
 b at a restaurant
 c at a party.

2 He'd like to buy her
 a a meal
 b a drink
 c a souvenir.

3 She gives him
 a her address
 b her phone number
 c her husband's phone number.

4 He'd like to phone her
 a at the weekend
 b on Sunday afternoon
 c on Monday morning.

GRAMMAR

1 Was Sie beim Abschied sagen können:

Was liegt am Ende des Buches näher, als Abschied zu nehmen. Und Abschied nehmen Sie im Englischen mit:

It was nice to see you again.	Es war nett, Dich/Euch/ Sie wiederzusehen.
It was lovely to meet you.	Es war schön, Dich/Euch/ Sie kennenzulernen.
Say goodbye to ... for us.	Sag/Sagt/Sagen Sie ... in unserem Namen auf Wiedersehen.
Have a good trip.	Gute Reise/Fahrt.
See you again next year.	Bis nächstes Jahr. / Auf Wiedersehen im nächsten Jahr.
Goodbye everyone.	Auf Wiedersehen allerseits.
Thanks for everything.	Danke für alles.

2 Wie Sie ausdrücken, daß Sie etwas 'unbedingt' tun müssen: / Wie Sie jemandem etwas nachdrücklich empfehlen:

I must go home now.
Ich muß jetzt nach Hause gehen.

You must see the film.
Sie müssen den Film sehen.

Stellen Sie hinter das Hilfsverb *must* das gewünschte Verb in seiner Grundform ohne *to*.

3 Das englische Alphabet:

A [eɪ]	F [ef]	K [keɪ]	P [pi:]	U [ju:]
B [bi:]	G [dʒi:]	L [el]	Q [kju:]	V [vi:]
C [si:]	H [eɪtʃ]	M [em]	R [ɑ:]	W ['dʌblju:]
D [di:]	I [aɪ]	N [en]	S [es]	X [eks]
E [i:]	J [dʒeɪ]	O [əʊ]	T [ti:]	Y [waɪ]

Z = britisches Englisch [zed]; amerikanisches Englisch [zi:]

[eɪ]	A, H, J, K
[i:]	B, C, D, E, G, P, T, V, (Z)
[e]	F, L, M, N, S, X, (Z)
[aɪ]	I, Y
[ju:]	Q,U,W

1 Make sentences with 'must'.

see go meet have say come

1 London is so exciting. You must go there.
2 The film's great. You .... it.
3 She'd like Hamburg. She .... and see us.
4 The weather's lovely. We .... a picnic.
5 She's not very well. She .... to bed early.
6 The taxi's here. I .... goodbye.
7 They don't know John. They .... him.

2 Find the letters.

Look at the code for activity 2, page 113.

20 12 12 23 25 2 22. 19 26 5 22 26 20 12 12 23 7 9 18 11. 11 15 22 26 8 22 8 22 13 23 6 8 26 11 12 8 7 24 26 9 23.

3 And now you.

Can you write a thank you card to your friends? You (and your family) stayed with friends for two weeks at their home. You went on three interesting trips with them. Look at page 104 for help.

Start like this:

Dear ...

HOMESTUDY

Lerntip

Versäumen Sie es nicht, das Alphabet auf Englisch zu lernen, damit Sie Ihren Namen, Ihre Anschrift oder was auch immer buchstabieren können. Achten Sie dabei vor allem auf den Unterschied zwischen a, e und i sowie zwischen g und j. Lassen Sie sich nicht sofort entmutigen, wenn es nicht gleich klappt. Im nächsten Kurs, mit dem Lehrwerk English Network 1, werden wir neben anderen wichtigen Dingen auch das Alphabet noch ausführlich üben. Bis dann können Sie sich in den Sommerferien für das neue Semester mit ***English Network Starter Break*** *rüsten!*

1 What is right?

(M = Midori, R = Hotel receptionist)
R: Good morning. Can/Must I help you?
M: I'd like to stay/live for two weeks.
R: With breakfast?
M: Yes, with breakfast.
R: Can I have your/her name, please?
M: Midori Wilson.
R: Can you spell/say that, please?
M: M-I-D-O-R-I Wilson.
R: Midori, that's not an/a English name.
M: No, it wasn't/isn't. My husband's English but Midori is a Japanese name.
R: It's a nice name. What does it/he mean?
M: It means/mean green.
R: That's interesting. Well, Mrs Wilson, here's his/the key for number 15.
M: Thank you.
R: You're welcome.

2 Please match.

1 I don't understand this word.
2 I don't know how to spell it.
3 I don't know where you live.
4 I don't know Hamburg.
5 I don't know Mrs Wilson.

☐ a Can I have your address?
☐ b You must come and visit us.
☐ c Can you spell it for me, please.
☐ d You must meet her.
☐ e What does it mean?

3 Reading

When you are in **King's Lynn** and would like information about the town and about interesting places to visit you can go to the **Tourist Information Office**. The Office is next to the Town Hall and opposite St Margaret's Church. The people who work at the Office are very friendly and the service is very good. But a hundred years ago the people were not very friendly and the service was awful. A hundred years ago it was the gaol!

What's right?

1 The Tourist Information Office is:
a in the Town Hall
b in St Margaret's Church
c next to the Town Hall.

2 The people who work there are:
a interesting
b awful
c friendly.

3 A hundred years ago it was:
a a hotel
b a post office
c a gaol.

4 Say it in English.

1 Sagen Sie, daß die Party Ihnen gut gefallen hat.
2 Danken Sie Ihrer Gastgeberin für alles, was sie getan hat.
3 Bitten Sie sie, den anderen Gästen in Ihrem Namen auf Wiedersehen zu sagen.
4 Sagen Sie, daß Ihre Gastgeberin Sie unbedingt besuchen muß.
5 Sagen Sie, daß es eine Freude war, sie kennenzulernen.

REVISION AND EXTENSION

• Starter

Look at the picture. What can Barry and Sally say?

Barry: I'd like to …
Sally: I'd ...

1 Stop: A spelling game

Ein Kursmitglied denkt sich ein Wort aus und malt soviele Striche, wie das Wort Buchstaben hat, an die Tafel, z.B. für das Wort 'orange' sechs Striche: _ _ _ _ _ _. Die anderen Kursmitglieder versuchen, das Wort zu erraten. Sie stellen Fragen wie: *Has it got a g*?. Enthält das Wort diesen Buchstaben, wird er an die entsprechende Stelle eingetragen: _ _ _ _ g _. Enthält es ihn nicht, wird der erste Strich eines Kastens um das Wort Stop gemalt. Die Klasse muß das Wort erraten, ehe das STOP-Schild fertig ist.

2 Your class list

Questions		Names	
have an exciting day yesterday?	Jim ✘	Chris ✔	Jane ✔
happy today?			
would like to go for a drink after class?			
enjoy the English class?			
would like to come to the English class next year?			

Look at the class list. Write the 5 questions. Use *Are/Do/Did/Would*

Example: Did you have an exciting day yesterday?

Now ask 3 students your questions. Write their names in the list. Note down their answers with ✔ or ✘.

✔ =	Yes, I am.	✘ =	No, I'm not.
	Yes, I do.		No, I don't.
	Yes, I did.		No, I didn't.
	Yes, I would		No, I wouldn't.

Then tell your class like this:
Chris and Jane had an exciting day but Jim didn't have an exciting day yesterday. ...

3 Complete with the letter E.

1 ic-cram ...	4 lttr ...	7 vry ...
2 ky ...	5 rally ...	8 whr ...
3 popl ...	6 dar ...	9 plas ...

4 The 'Things In Your Life' game

Würfeln Sie eine Zahl mit einem, zwei oder drei Würfeln. Erzählen Sie der Klasse etwas aus Ihrem Leben, was die entsprechende Anzahl von Jahren zurückliegt, z.B. 7 = vor 7 Jahren, 15 = vor 15 Jahren.

REVISION AND EXTENSION

5 Picture story

Work in groups of 4. Look at the pictures. Number the pictures 1– 5. Then write the story in your group.

Then tell your class your story.

6 And now you.

Write down 3-5 things for next year. Then tell your partner.

Next year I'd like ...
And then I ...

7 Memory check

What words from Unit 6 do you remember? Write them down. What were your partner's words?

8 Reading

Picnics are an English tradition and English people love picnics. In the summer they often pack a basket with sandwiches, apples, bananas, biscuits, tea or coffee, lemonade, coke or beer and go out into the country. Or they go to a park and sit in the grass and enjoy their food and drinks. They sometimes play ball or frisbee, too.

Sometimes they go to a cricket match and sit on the grass and have a picnic and watch the game. And sometimes people go to the sea and have a picnic in the car.

Option:
Write a letter to your teacher about things people do in your country.

• Useful phrases

Extra 3

Song

In the summer

Listen and complete.

I ..... you in the summer
On the first of July in
a ..... cafe
Wednesday .....
The first day of my .....
I'd like to ..... you again
I don't mind ..... or .....
Maybe ..... summer in
the ..... cafe
Same ....., same .....
Let's ..... again next summer
I'll be there ..... the first
of July
In the .....
And next time don't say ..... .

Crossword

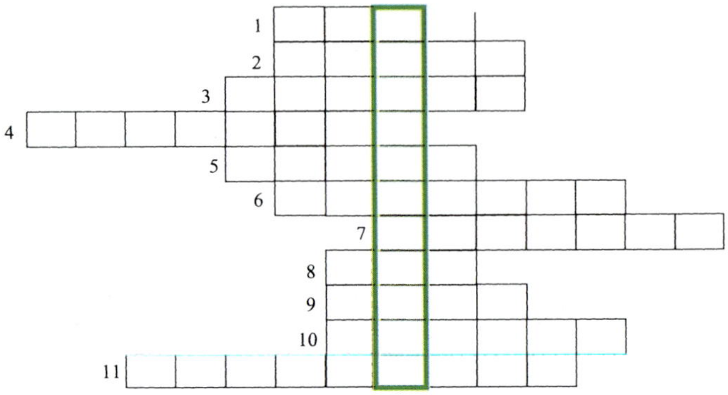

1 Where did you go on holiday ..... year?
2 Edinburgh! Can you ..... that, please?
3 I saw a good film at the ..... yesterday.
4 The people at the bed-and-breakfast were very ..... .
5 Did you ..... your trip to Wales?
6 England is an interesting ..... .
7 What's your ..... in Bristol?
8 She started her English class two years ..... .
9 Can you ..... me the biscuits, please?
10 It's a lovely day. Let's have a ..... .
11 Have you got a lot of ..... for your friends?

The mystery sentence is: ___ ___ _____ .

Abbreviation Bingo

BBC	FBI
KLM	AI
CIA	TWA
UFO	KGB
ITV	NBC
SAS	JAL
AFN	GB
HRH	USA

Schreiben Sie die 16 Abkürzungen in die Kästchen, jedoch nicht in der vorgegebenen Reihenfolge. Ihr Kursleiter / Ihre Kursleiterin liest sie dann in beliebiger Reihenfolge vor. Streichen Sie sie nacheinander durch. Wer zuerst eine Reihe (senkrecht, waagerecht oder diagonal) durchgestrichen hat, ruft 'Bingo' und hat gewonnen.

Extra 3

Spotlight

Edinburgh–a wonderful place

Most tourists visit London. But not a lot go to Edinburgh, the capital of Scotland. Edinburgh is a beautiful city, with a lovely old castle.

The main street is Princes Street. It has got a lot of shops on one side, and parks and monuments on the other side. From Princes Street you can always see the castle on the hill. It's marvellous.

Every year in the summer there is the Edinburgh International Festival. Then Edinburgh is very crowded. People come from Japan and Australia, from Germany and Italy – from all over the world. It is a big cultural event. You can meet a lot of interesting people and see a lot of interesting things. In the streets, in the parks, in the theatres, in the restaurants and in the pubs. Edinburgh at festival time is an exciting place.

A Quiz

✔ = yes ✘ = no

- ☐ 1 King's Lynn has got a Monday Market Place and a Thursday Market Place.
- ☐ 2 In England, corner shops are often open on Sunday, too.
- ☐ 3 There are flying doctors in Australia.
- ☐ 4 English people like picnics.
- ☐ 5 There is a transport museum in Cambridge.
- ☐ 6 Bed-and-breakfast places are awful hotels.
- ☐ 7 Number 10, Downing Street is in London.
- ☐ 8 The Edinburgh Festival is always in winter.
- ☐ 9 There is a river with punts in Cambridge.

Übungsanweisungen für Partner B in den Übungen *Exchange information with your partner*

Unit 2 Step 1, Activity 3a, Seite 29: Partner B

B. You are Jane/James Thomas. This is your house. Ask A questions and answer A's questions. Example:

– Have you got a television?
– Yes, we have. / No, we haven't.
– Have you got ...?
– ...

OK? Now tell A what you haven't got:
You've got ... in your house, but we haven't got ...

Unit 2 Step 2, Activity 2b, Seite 33: Partner B

It is summer. Where are Mark and Tina's friends? Ask A questions and answer A's questions.
Example:
– Where is Dennis?
– He's in Marbella.
– Where are Carmen and Glenn?
– They're in Lugano.

Dennis	Marbella
Barbara	?
Sven + Anita	?
Carmen + Glenn	Lugano
Tom + Glenda	?

Unit 3 Step 1, Activity 2b, Seite 47: Partner B

You are in a shop in London. Ask A questions and write the answers:

How much is/are ...?

Unit 4 Step 2, Activity 1b, Seite 67: Partner B

Answer your partner's questions, then look at the box, and ask your partner questions:
How often do you ...?

	never	sometimes	often	usually	always
drink coffee for breakfast					
play tennis in summer					
read the newspaper					
go to a museum					
eat ice-cream in winter					
go to bed early					
get up at 10.00					

Unit 4 Step 3, Activity 2a, Seite 71: Partner B

You work for the tourist information office. Answer A's questions.

British Museum	10.00 am - 5.00 pm
Madame Tussaud's	10.00 am - 6.00 pm
London Transport Museum	10.00 am - 6.00 pm
Wimbledon Tennis Museum	11.00 am - 5.00 pm
Houses of Parliament	10.00 am - 1.30 pm
Tower of London	9.30 am - 5.00 pm

Unit 5 Step 1, Activity 2b, Seite 81: Partner B

You and A organised an international party on Saturday. But where were the guests? It wasn't the right day! Now it's Monday. Answer A's questions, ask A questions.

Vanessa	with a friend in Norwich
Helen	?
Norman	?
John	at work
Karel	?
Astrid + Sven	in Hyde Park
the Wilsons	?
Tina + Mark	in Colchester

Example:
A: Where was Vanessa?
B: She was with a friend in Norwich.

Unit 6 Step 3, Activity 2, Seite 105: Partner B

This is a code. A has got two sentences, but in numbers, not letters. A tells you the numbers. You tell A the letters. What are A's sentences?

26	25	24	23	22	21	20	19	18	17	16	15	14
A	B	C	D	E	F	G	H	I	J	K	L	M

13	12	11	10	9	8	7	6	5	4	3	2	1
N	O	P	Q	R	S	T	U	V	W	X	Y	Z

Unit 1 Step 1

1. are, Hello, fine, this, is, Hello, Nice, meet
2. 1 this, 2 hello, 3 are, 4 fine, 5 thanks, 6 is.
   Lösungswort: thanks
3. 1-b, 2-c, 3-a
4. 1-c, 2-e, 3-a, 4-b, 5-d

Unit 1 Step 2

1. 1 A cup of tea, please. 2 An orange, please.
   3 A banana, please. 4 An ice-cream, please.
   5 A sandwich, please.
2. H: Have a cup of tea. – M: Thank you.
   – H: And a biscuit? – M: No, thanks.
3. 1-f, 2-c, 3-d, 4-e, 5-b, 6-a
4. 1-e, 2-a, 3-b, 4-d, 5-c

Unit 1 Step 3

1. 1 F, 2 T, 3 F, 4 T, 5 F
2. 1 for, 2 to, 3 from, 4 in, of, 5 for
3. 1-d, 2-e, 3-a, 4-b, 5-c
4. are, 'm, Is, isn't, 's, are, am, 'm
5. for - four, nine - fine, three - tea, ice - nice, you - two, seat - meet
6. 1-e, 2-d, 3-c, 4-b, 5-a

Unit 1, Revision and Extension

Starter. A banana, an orange, an apple, a sandwich, a cup of tea, a biscuit, a telephone, a key

1. How, you, Hello, fine, And, are, thanks, this is, this is, Hello, Hello, Nice, meet

3. 1-c, 2-f, 3-e, 4-b, 5-g, 6-d, 7-a

4. a two, b seven, c nine, d three, e eight, f five, g four, h six, i one

6.

Q	O	W	H	E	R	E	Z	E
E	S	E	A	T	Y	O	U	R
M	M	L	E	P	H	O	N	E
N	I	C	E	T	M	E	E	T
F	R	O	M	S	F	I	N	E
C	O	M	E	V	I	T	U	I
P	L	E	A	S	E	C	O	V

Unit 2 Step 1

1. Across: 1 problem, 2 television, 5 dictionary
   Down: 1 photo, 3 video, 4 key, 6 tea
2. 1-e, 2-a, 3-d, 4-b, 5-c
3. 1 Really? 2 Never mind. 3 Good. 4 You're welcome.

Unit 2 Step 2

1. your, her, my, his

2.

F	A	T	H	E	R	T	U	R	A	F
T	A	B	W	G	C	A	V	M	B	N
M	H	A	W	I	F	E	K	B	L	H
O	O	E	R	O	T	H	O	R	C	U
T	T	B	L	E	T	S	R	O	N	S
H	H	T	S	S	O	N	U	T	S	B
E	L	L	P	U	A	N	T	H	O	A
R	O	S	I	S	T	E	R	E	E	N
S	A	D	D	B	I	C	H	R	D	D
N	N	E	D	A	U	G	H	T	E	R

3. is, 're, got, my, his, son, wife, got, Her
4. 1-e, 2-c, 3-d, 4-a, 5-b

Unit 2 Step 3

1. 1 Vanessa, 2 Norman, 3 Karen, 4 Tina
2. 1 hairdryer, 2 thanks, 3 key, 4 student, 5 dictionary, 6 who, 7 London

3. 2 She hasn't got a computer. 3 She hasn't got a hotel. 4 She's got four hats. 5 She's got five friends.

4. 1-d, 2-e, 3-c, 4-a, 5-b

Unit 2 Revision and Extension

Starter. He's got a hotel / a computer / a video camera / a shop / a swimming pool / a (nice) house.

1. have, haven't, have, have, have got, haven't got, have got.

6. 2 He's my son. 3 She's my daughter. 4 She's my mother. 5 He's my brother. 6 She's my sister. 7 He's my father.

Extra 1

Song. Seven, seven, one-two-seven, seven-four-seven, seven, seven, one-three-five-eight-nine

Crossword. 1 dictionary, 2 husband, 3 meet, 4 never, 5 near, 6 please, 7 let's, 8 but, 9 fine, 10 number, 11 Germany

Odd man out. 2 dictionary, 3 drink, 4 coffee, 5 awful

Unit 3 Step 1

1. 1-d, 2-a, 3-b, 4-c

2. ninety-nine pounds ninety-nine, fifty-one pounds fifty-five

3. 1 Who are they? 2 Where is he? 3 How is she? 4 What has he got? 5 How much is the map?

4. next to, opposite, in, in, on

5. 1-c How much is the postcard? 2-a How much are the stamps? 3-d Where is the nearest post office, please? 4-b Have you got a map of King's Lynn?

Unit 3 Step 2

1. afternoon, do, in, Do, don't, has, close

2. 1 Do they work for a computer firm? No, they don't. 2 Do they work for a bank? Yes, they do. 3 Do they like English food? Yes, they do. 4 Do they drink coke? No they don't. 5 Do they go to discos? Yes, they do. 6 Do they go to pubs? No, they don't. 7 Do they eat hamburgers? Yes, they do.

3. 1-b, 2-e, 3-d, 4-c, 5-a

Unit 3 Step 3

1. When, Where, Where, Do, don't, don't

2. Wednesday, Thursday, Tuesday, Monday, Sunday, Friday, Saturday.

3. They go to the pub on Wednesday evening. They go to the disco on Thursday evening. They play squash on Friday at 4 o'clock. They play tennis on Saturday at 11 o'clock. They go to the park on Sunday morning.

4. 1-d, 2-g, 3-f, 4-b, 5-c, 6-a, 7-e

5. 1-c, 2-e, 3-d, 4-a, 5-b

Unit 4 Step 1

1. works, lives, speaks, goes, likes, eats.

2. 1 Yes, he does. 2 Yes, she does. 3 No, he doesn't. 4 No, she doesn't. 5 Yes, he does.

3. 1 ... lives in Australia. 2 ... their son is a flying doctor. 3 ... their daughter's name is Vanessa. 4 ... their son's name is John. 5 ... their daughter lives in Australia. 6 ... their son lives in Tokyo.

4. 1-d, 2-a, 3-b, 4-e, 5-c

Unit 4 Step 2

1. lives, works, reads, starts, speaks, doesn't speak, gets up, doesn't work, doesn't read, likes, plays, doesn't play, likes, goes, likes, doesn't like.

2. 1 weather, 2 early, 3 weekend, 4 too, 5 get up, 6 friend, 7 street

3. 3 That's OK. You're not late. 1 It's at nine o'clock. 2 Oh, that's early. Why so early?

4. 1 Does she work a lot? 2 Does she work at the weekend? 3 Does she read the news? 4 Does she get up early? 5 Does she go to bed late? 6 Does she speak German?

Unit 4 Step 3

1. When does she start work? When does she get up? What time does she come home? How does she come home?
2. on, in, with, In, by, On, to, for, from.
3. 1 leaves, 2 hotel, 3 train, 4 next, 5 holiday, 6 to, 7 in
4. 1-b, 2-e, 3-d, 4-a, 5-c

Unit 4 Revision and Extension

1. 1-e, 2-a, 3-c, 4-b, 5-d
3. 2 Tuesday, 3 Friday, 4 Monday, 5 Saturday, 6 Thursday
4. live, works, is, get up, have, leaves, reads, goes, works, starts, comes, starts, doesn't work, meets, goes

Extra 2

Song. two, start, late, always, leave, arrive, summer, winter, train, train, two, start, car, never, sometimes, work, leave, arrive, summer, winter, train, train, sometimes, train

Crossword. 1 with, 2 doctor, 3 early, 4 train, 5 understand, 6 walk, 7 play, 8 close, 9 stamp, 10 arrives, 11 nearest, 12 left, 13 Sunday, 14 winter

What's my name? 1 Arnold Schwarzenegger, 2 Mona Lisa

Who is 00 Buzz? James Bond

Unit 5 Step 1

1. were, was, was, were, were, was, was.
2. 1-c, 2-e, 3-a, 4-b, 5-d
3. day, meal, restaurant, weather, afternoon, river, boat, first, suddenly, water.
4. What was your day like? It wasn't very nice. Why was that? I wasn't very well. How are you now? I'm fine thanks.

Unit 5 Step 2

1. hired, travelled, arrived, camped, played, rained, visited, enjoyed.
2. We hired a car. We stayed with my sister in Toronto. We visited Niagara Falls. We travelled to Quebec. We camped near Lake Huron.
3. I started my first job in 1985. In a German restaurant in London. Oh, yes I did, very much. I opened a restaurant. I opened it in 1989. I am very happy now. It's great.
4. 1-d, 2-e, 3-a, 4-c, 5-b

Unit 5 Step 3

2. 1 She had lunch with Nicola on Wednesday. 2 They had lunch in a lovely restaurant near the office. 3 She didn't have lunch. She worked in the office. 4 The weather was awful. 5 She was tired. 6 She went to the cinema with Nicola. 7 They saw "Batman". 8 She went with her mother to visit her sister. 9 Tim wasn't there. 10 She wasn't well.

3.

S	A	W	T	A	B	L	E	P	A
T	R	A	D	E	H	W	J	L	E
R	O	S	C	A	M	E	L	A	D
A	N	O	P	E	T	N	Y	Y	S
V	A	P	S	O	N	T	K	E	T
E	R	E	N	J	O	Y	E	D	A
L	O	N	D	O	N	A	D	A	R
L	A	E	T	H	A	D	F	U	T
E	L	D	E	R	A	B	B	I	E
D	E	A	R	O	H	I	R	E	D

4. 1 Did you have lunch in a pub? 2 Did you enjoy the tour? 3 Did you see everything? 4 Did you stay there all day? 5 Did you come home late?

Unit 5 Revision and Extension

1. morning - evening, last week - next week, come - go, lovely - awful, early - late, arrive - leave, night - day, summer - winter, always - never

2. 1 Last summer we travelled to Scotland. 2 We went there by train. 3 Edinburgh was very exciting. 4 We saw a lot of interesting streets. 5 It didn't rain very often in Scotland. 6 We hired a car for two days. 7 It was a lovely summer holiday.

Unit 6 Step 1

2. 1 She meets a lot of interesting people from different countries. 2 They come from all over Europe. 3 No, he didn't. 4 She started the business 13 years ago. 5 She was only two. 6 It was awful. 7 He works for a garage in King's Lynn.

3. Work: business, full-time, job, firm. Sport: game, squash, play, ice hockey. Holiday: B&B, travel, postcard, camp.

4. When were you born? When did you get married? When did you meet your wife? When was your daughter born?

Unit 6 Step 2

1. Across: 3 enjoyed, 5 was, 7 hired.
   Down: 1 bought, 2 met, 4 had, 5 went, 6 saw.

2. 1 you, us, us, us, them. 2 it, you, us.

3. 1 Can I take a photo of you, please? 2 Can I have the ketchup, please? 3 Can I see you again, please? 4 Can we have/play a game of tennis, please? 5 Can I speak to Helen, please?

4. 1 Can you pass me the biscuits, please? 2 I'd like a sandwich, too, please. 3 Here you are. 4 What do you think of Norfolk? 5 Can I take a photo of you, please?

Unit 6 Step 3

1. Can I help you? I'd like to stay for 2 weeks. Can I have your name, please? Can you spell that, please? Midori, that's not an English name. No, it isn't. What does it mean? It means green. Here's the key for number 15.

2. 1-e, 2-c, 3-a, 4-b, 5-d

3. 1-c, 2-c, 3-c

4. 1 I enjoyed the party. 2 Thanks for everything. 3 Please say goodbye to all the guests for us. 4 You must come and visit us/me. 5 It was lovely to meet you.

Unit 6 Revision and Extension

3. 1 ice-cream, 2 key, 3 people, 4 letter, 5 really, 6 dear, 7 very, 8 where, 9 please

Extra 3

Song. met, small, morning, holiday, meet, where, when, next, small, time, place, meet, on, morning, goodbye

Crossword. 1 last, 2 spell, 3 cinema, 4 friendly, 5 enjoy, 6 country, 7 address, 8 ago, 9 pass, 10 picnic, 11 souvenirs

Abbreviation bingo. Die Abkürzungen stehen für folgende Organisationen: BBC *British Broadcasting Corporation*, halbstaatlicher britischer Fernseh- und Rundfunksender; KLM holländische Fluggesellschaft; CIA *Central Intelligence Agency*, amerikanischer Geheimdienst; UFO *unidentified flying object*, nicht identifiziertes Flugobjekt; ITV *Independent Television*, Gruppe britischer Privatfernsehsender; SAS *Scandinavian Airlines*, skandinavische Fluggesellschaft; AFN *American Forces Network*, Rundfunksender für amerikanische Stationierungstruppen im Ausland; HRH *Her/His Royal Highness* = ihre/seine königliche Hoheit; FBI *Federal Bureau of Investigation*, amerikanische Bundespolizei; AI *Amnesty International*, internationale Gefangenenhilfe-Organisation; TWA *Trans World Airlines*, amerikanische Fluggesellschaft; KGB sowjetischer Geheimdienst; NBC *National Broadcasting Corporation*, amerikanischer Fernsehsender; JAL *Japan Airlines*, japanische Fluggesellschaft; GB *Great Britain*, Großbritannien; USA *United States of America*, Vereinigte Staaten von Amerika.

A Quiz. 2, 3, 4, 7, 9 sind richtig.

In dieser Rubrik finden Sie Informationen über das Leben in Großbritannien und was dort anders ist. Damit wird der Hintergrund einiger Dialogszenen im Buch erläutert. Gleichzeitig finden Sie Tips, wie man sich in bestimmten Situationen verhält und können damit mögliche 'Fettnäpfchen' vermeiden.

Unit 1, Step 1, Activity 3b

Tina macht Mark und Helen miteinander bekannt und benutzt dabei nur die Vornamen. In Großbritannien und Amerika werden sie im beruflichen und im privaten Bereich bereitwillig verwendet, der Gebrauch der Familiennamen ist seltener. Warten Sie jedoch bitte, bis man Sie mit dem Vornamen anredet, denn sonst könnte u. U. Ihr 'Vorpreschen' als anbiedernd empfunden werden.
Mark und Helen geben sich beim Kennenlernen die Hand. Seien Sie aber nicht erstaunt, wenn Sie Engländer oder Amerikaner zum ersten Male treffen, und man Ihnen nicht sofort herzhaft die Hand schüttelt. Es sei denn, Sie werden einander offiziell vorgestellt. Bei einem Wiedersehen wird ebenfalls oft auf das Händeschütteln verzichtet. Das alles soll Sie nicht verunsichern, lassen Sie doch Ihr Gegenüber den ersten Schritt tun, da es für den 'Handshake' keine klaren Regeln gibt.

Unit 1, Step 2, Dialogue

Tee ist noch immer das britische Nationalgetränk, obwohl heute immer mehr Kaffee – wenn auch oft nur Pulverkaffee – getrunken wird. Häufig wird man Ihnen bei einem Besuch eine Tasse Tee oder Kaffee anbieten, wenn man Sie nicht zum Essen eingeladen hat. Die Engländer trinken ihren Tee mit Milch; wenn Sie das nicht mögen, sagen Sie es bitte gleich, denn sonst wird Ihnen ein Getränk serviert, an dessen Farbe und Geschmack Sie sich gewöhnen müssen. Wenn man Sie nachmittags so gegen vier Uhr zum Tee einlädt, bedeutet das eine kleine Mahlzeit, bei der Sie neben dem Tee ganz sicher auch eine Kleinigkeit zu essen gereicht bekommen werden. *Tea* im Norden Englands gegen sechs Uhr ist eine reichhaltige, dem Abendessen vergleichbare Mahlzeit.

Unit 1, Step 3, Dialogue Part 1

Norman ist stolz darauf, Waliser zu sein (aus Wales zu stammen). Er hört es nicht gern, als Engländer bezeichnet zu werden. Zunächst ist er Waliser, erst in zweiter Linie Brite. Das gleiche gilt auch für die Schotten und Iren. Und auch die Amerikaner und Kanadier, die Australier und Neuseeländer wollen nicht gern in einen Topf geworfen werden.

Unit 1, Step 3, Dialogue Part 3

Rufen Sie in Großbritannien jemand an, so wird man sich meistens nicht mit dem Namen melden, sondern mit der Telefonnummer. Im Geschäftsverkehr wird jedoch meist der Firmenname genannt.

Unit 2, Step 1, Activity 3a

Eines Engländers Heim ist sein 'Schloß', ganz gleich wie es aussehen mag oder in welchem Zustand es ist. Sie werden sehr bald feststellen, daß deutsche Vorstellungen hinsichtlich Ausstattung und Komfort nicht von allen Engländern geteilt werden. Fernseher und Videogerät sind häufig vorhanden, doch haben die Häuser z.B. oft keine Isolierverglasung und manchmal keine Zentralheizung. Denken Sie bitte daran, Adapter für die Steckdosen mitzunehmen.
Anmerkung: Im Badezimmer gibt es keine Steckdosen, folglich können Sie Ihren Haartrockner dort nicht benutzen. Und häufig werden Sie auch noch eine Dusche vergeblich suchen: eine Badewanne ist die Standardausrüstung.

Unit 2, Step 2, Activity 3c

Wie oben schon festgehalten wurde, meldet man sich in Großbritannien am Telefon meist nur mit der Telefonnummer. In unserem Telefondialog fügt die Angerufene ihren Namen hinzu (*This is Evelyn Jones*). Als Anrufende(r) sollten Sie erst Ihren Namen sagen, wenn Sie danach gefragt werden (*Who's calling, please? / Who's speaking, please?*).

Unit 3, Step 1, Dialogue

100 Pence sind 1 Pfund (= £1. Achten Sie übrigens darauf, daß beim Schreiben zwischen dem Pfundsymbol £ und der nachfolgenden Zahl kein Zwischenraum vorhanden ist.) Das Pfund ist eine Münze. Es gibt 5-, 10-, 20- und 50-Pfund-Noten. Der bargeldlose Zahlungsverkehr ist in Großbritannien und Amerika weit verbreitet, in Supermärkten und Geschäften und auch am Bahnhofsschalter wird oft mit Schecks oder Kreditkarten bezahlt.

Unit 3, Step 2, Dialogue Part 3

In Großbritannien werden die Öffnungszeiten von Gaststätten und Kneipen ('Gott sei Dank!' haben viele Stammgäste, die 'regulars', gesagt) zunehmend freizügiger gehandhabt. Viele von Ihnen sind von 11 Uhr morgens bis Mitternacht geöffnet. Darauf sollten Sie sich jedoch nicht verlassen, sondern lieber selber nachschauen, ob nicht einige Gaststätten besondere Schließzeiten haben.
In der Kneipe wird der Gast nie für sich allein ein Getränk bestellen, sondern, wie John im Dialog, auch für seine Begleitung ('eine Runde geben'). Diesem Beispiel sollten Sie unbedingt folgen, um nicht als knauserig angesehen zu werden. In Kneipen können Sie auch etwas essen: preiswerte Gerichte, heiß oder kalt. In Begleitung ihrer Eltern dürfen auch Kinder in die Kneipe, bekommen dort aber selbstverständlich keine alkoholischen Getränke.

Unit 3, Step 2, Homestudy

Die Geschäfte in Großbritannien sind gewöhnlich von 9 bis 17 Uhr oder 17.30 geöffnet, wobei einige auch über die Mittagszeit schließen. In Vorstädten oder kleineren Orten sind die Geschäfte oft an einem Wochentag nur halbtags geöffnet. Große Ketten haben häufig einen Abend in der Woche oder sogar mehrere bis in die Abendstunden auf. Der kleine Laden in der Nachbarschaft (Tante Emma-Laden), der Zeitungskiosk, Läden, die von Einwanderern geführt werden, sind oft länger geöffnet und stehen Ihnen auch an Sonn- und Feiertagen offen. Alle Geschäfte sind am Samstagnachmittag offen. In den Vereinigten Staaten von Amerika gibt es kaum geregelte Ladenschlußzeiten, die Geschäftsbesitzer können selbst bestimmen, wann sie für ihre Kundschaft da sind.

Unit 4, Step 2, Dialogue

Breakfast heißt für die meisten Briten heutzutage Cornflakes oder Müsli, Toast und Orangenmarmelade, Tee oder Kaffee. In *Bed-and-Breakfast*-Unterkünften und in Hotels (oft gegen Aufpreis) bekommt man noch das traditionelle *English breakfast*: Cornflakes, Schinkenspeck oder Würstchen mit Rühr- bzw. Spiegeleiern oder sogar Fisch. Haben Sie das verdaut, packen Sie noch Toast und Marmelade obendrauf, selbstverständlich in dieser Reihenfolge. Guten Appetit!

Unit 4, Step 2, Homestudy

Bed-and-Breakfast-Unterkünfte sind preiswerter als Hotels und werden meist von Privatpersonen geführt. Ihre Atmosphäre ist freundlich und anheimelnd; sie bieten zudem noch den Vorteil, daß Sie Ihr Englisch anwenden und die britische Lebensart kennenlernen können. Wollen Sie mit Ihrem Reisebegleiter / Ihrer Reisebegleiterin 'das Bettuch' teilen, wählen Sie das *double bed*, sonst sollten Sie für eine ungestörte Nachtruhe *twin beds* vorziehen.

Unit 5, Step 3, Activity 3c

Die Sehenswürdigkeiten in einer Großstadt wie London liegen weit auseinander, so ist es wirklich eine gute Idee, eine Busrundfahrt zu machen, um einen Überblick zu gewinnen, und erst danach die Sie interessierenden Stätten zu besuchen. Das haben auch Mark und Tina gemacht.

Unit 6, Step 1, Dialogue

Helen berichtet, daß sie und Norman ein großes Haus hatten/haben, obwohl sie nicht besonders wohlhabend sein dürften. Die Anzahl der Hauseigentümer ist in Großbritannien im Vergleich zu den deutschsprachigen Ländern erstaunlich hoch, wenn man bedenkt, daß Großbritanniens Lebensstandard im EG-Vergleich sonst eher niedriger ist. Das liegt daran, daß junge Paare das eigene Haus als das Ideale ansehen, sei es auch noch so bescheiden, und das System der Bausparkassenfinanzierung es ermöglicht, daß auch Menschen mit niedrigerem Einkommen Hausbesitz erwerben können. Wenn wir einmal von Luxusappartements in London und anderen bedeutenden Großstädten absehen, so werden Wohnungen in der Regel als weniger erstrebenswert und als eine Art 'Übergangslösung' betrachtet. Deshalb wird es auch manche Briten erstaunen, wenn sie erfahren, daß Sie in einer Wohnung leben. Diese Ansichten verändern sich jedoch allmählich, schon allein durch den Druck der (finanziellen) Verhältnisse.

Unit 6, Step 3, Activity 1

Bei den Adressen steht in Großbritannien und in Amerika die Hausnummer an erster Stelle, d.h. vor dem Straßennamen. Vergessen Sie bitte auch nicht, die Postleitzahl in eine eigene Zeile zu schreiben. Die Postleitzahl in Großbritannien (*postcode*) besteht aus einer komplizierten Kombination von Buchstaben und Ziffern und hat oft keine erkennbare Verbindung mit dem Ort (z.B. könnte sie für Throope leicht CN17 5SR heißen oder eine andere genauso wenig durchschaubare Kombination). Die Postleitzahlen in den USA (*zipcode*) bestehen aus einer Abkürzung für den Bundesstaat und einer mehrstelligen Zahl.

Unit 6, Step 3, Activity 3

Wenn Sie einem Engländer oder Amerikaner für etwas danken wollen, so sollten Sie dies ruhig 'überschwenglich' tun mit z.B. *Thank you very much for the meal. It was lovely. We really enjoyed it.* Es mag Ihnen vielleicht übertrieben vorkommen, doch ist es zweifellos besser, zu viel zu sagen als zu wenig. Allzu kurze Sätze und Aussagen werden in englischsprachigen Ländern oft als etwas unhöflich empfunden.

GRAMMATIKREGISTER UND -GLOSSAR

In diesem Register wird angegeben, wo die betreffende Grammatik mit Beispielsätzen und deutschsprachigen Erklärungen kommentiert wird. Als Fundstelle sind Unit und Step angegeben: so bedeutet z.B. 1/2, daß das Grammatikproblem in Unit 1 Step 2 auf der *Grammar*-Seite zu finden ist.

Grammatischer Begriff	Erklärung	Beispiele
Artikel (*article*)	Geschlechtswort Begleiter des Hauptworts	**a** cup of tea **an** ice-cream **the** coffee
Eigenschaftswörter (*adjectives*)	beschreiben Dinge, verleihen Gefühlen Ausdruck und sagen somit etwas über Hauptwörter (s. u.) aus	a **new** house an **exciting** game
Fragewörter (*question words*)	leiten häufig Fragesätze ein	**Where** is Silvia? **What** does she do at the weekend? **How** is she? **When** does she come?
Grundform (*infinitive*)	Nennform des Verbs, die im Wörterbuch steht, und die mit einem Hilfsverb auftritt	**see** You must **see** the film.
Haupt- oder Namenwörter (*nouns*)	geben Menschen, Tieren, Dingen und abstrakten Begriffen ihren Namen	**Peter** the **dog** the **pub** **holidays** **time**
Hilfszeitwörter verben (*auxiliaries*)	ermöglichen, Fragen zu bilden, Aussagen zu verneinen und Kurzantworten zu geben	– **Did** you visit the museum? oder - – No, I **did**n't. I **did**n't have the time.
Zeitwörter oder Verben (*verbs*)	beschreiben Tätigkeiten oder Zustände	We **like** London and **go** there every year.

LEITFADEN AUSSPRACHE

In den nachfolgenden Wortschatzanhängen *Vocabulary* und *Dictionary* wird die Aussprache in eckigen Klammern nach jedem Eintrag angegeben. Dazu wird eine spezielle Lautschrift verwendet, deren wichtigste Symbole hier erläutert werden.

Symbol	Beispielwort	Aussprache
ə	numb**er**	wie *e* in deutsch *singe*
ɪ	**i**n	wie *i* in deutsch *in*
ɪə	**here**	wie *ie* in deutsch *hier*
i:	m**ee**t	wie *ie* in deutsch *Knie*
e	y**e**s	etwa wie *e* in deutsch *fett*
eɪ	d**ay**	nicht wie deutsch *ei* sondern [e] + [ɪ]
eə	wh**ere**	wie *air* in deutsch *fair*
æ	th**a**nks	zwischen deutschem *a* und *ä*
aɪ	n**i**ce	wie *ei* in deutsch *Eile*
aʊ	h**ow**	wie *au* in deutsch *flau*
ɑ:	f**a**ther	wie *ah* in deutsch *Kahn*
ɒ	c**o**ffee	wie *o* in deutsch *Motte*
ɔɪ	b**oy**	wie *eu* in *deutsch*
ɔ:	f**our**	wie *o* in deutsch *Borke*
ʌ	c**o**me	wie *a* in deutsch *Klatsch*
ʊ	l**oo**k	wie *u* in deutsch *Butter*
ʊə	t**our**ist	[ʊ] + [ə]
əʊ	n**o**	[ə] + [ʊ]
u:	t**oo**	etwa wie *u* in deutsch *Tuch*
ɜ:	**ear**ly	etwa wie *ö* in deutsch *Segeltörn*
v	ha**v**e	wie *V* in deutsch *Virus*
θ	**th**anks	wie ein gelispeltes *ß* in deutsch *Biß*
ð	**th**is	wie ein gelispeltes *s* in deutsch *Sand*
s	**s**eat	wie *ß* in deutsch *Muße*
z	plea**s**e	wie *s* in deutsch *Museum*
ʃ	**sh**e	wie *sch* in deutsch *fesch*
ʒ	televi**s**ion	wie *g* in deutsch *Regie*
tʃ	**ch**eers	wie *tsch* in deutsch *Klatsch*
dʒ	**G**erman	[d] + [ʒ]
ŋ	so**ng**	wie *ng* in deutsch *singen*
r	**r**epeat	nicht wie ein deutsches *r*, sondern vorn im Munde gesprochen
w	**w**e	nicht wie ein deutsches *w*, sondern durch die Lippen wie [u:]
Der hochgestellte Strich ' steht in Wörtern mit mehr als einer Silbe vor dem Teil des Wortes, der am stärksten betont wird.		

VOCABULARY

Hier finden Sie eine Auflistung sämtlicher Wörter und Wendungen des Buches. Sie erscheinen in der Reihenfolge, wie sie vorne im Buch vorkommen.
In der linken Spalte steht jeweils das englische Wort oder die Wendung und dahinter in eckigen Klammern die Aussprache. Einen Leitfaden zur Aussprache finden Sie auf der Vorseite. In der nächsten Spalte erscheint die deutsche Übersetzung und in der rechten Spalte meist ein Satzbeispiel, in dem das englische Wort stehen könnte. Wenn Sie die Vokabeln einmal gelernt haben, können Sie diese rechte Spalte benutzen, um sich selber abzufragen. Sie decken dabei die linke Spalte zu und versuchen, die durch das Zeichen ~ markierte Lücke mit dem richtigen Wort zu füllen.

Die **fettgedruckten** Wörter und Wendungen sind besonders nützlich. Sie werden sie öfter brauchen und sollten sie deshalb vorrangig lernen. Die Wörter in normalem Druck sind in diesem Buch noch nicht so wichtig, daß Sie sie immer parat haben müssen. Es genügt, wenn Sie sie wiedererkennen können.
Wörter und Ausdrücke, die besonders häufig in den Übungsanweisungen und Überschriften vorkommen, finden Sie nicht hier im *Vocabulary*, sondern auf der Innenseite des Umschlags hinten.
Die Buchstaben im linken Rand des *Vocabulary* stehen für folgende Teile:

S = Starter	G = Grammar
I = Bildseite	H = Homestudy
D = Dialogue	U = Useful phrases
A = Activities	

STARTER

computer [kəm'pju:tə]	Computer
tennis ['tenɪs]	Tennis
hotel [həʊ'tel]	Hotel
T-shirt ['ti:ʃɜ:t]	T-Shirt
mountain bike ['maʊntɪn baɪk]	Mountainbike
squash [skwɒʃ]	Squash
video ['vɪdɪəʊ]	Video
bank [bæŋk]	Bank
sandwich ['sænwɪdʒ]	Sandwich; belegtes Brot
hamburger ['hæmbɜ:gə]	Hamburger
park [pɑ:k]	Park
jeans [dʒi:nz]	Jeans
steak [steɪk]	Steak
sweatshirt ['swetʃɜ:t]	Sweatshirt
golf [gɒlf]	Golf

UNIT 1

I	arrival [ə'raɪvl]	Ankunft
	population [ˌpɒpjʊ'leɪʃn]	Bevölkerung

UNIT 1 *Step 1*

S	**hello** [hə'ləʊ]	Guten Tag; Grüß Gott; Grüezi; Hallo	~ Tina, – ~ Helen.
D	**I** [aɪ]	ich	
	'm (= am) [m/æm]	bin	
	I'm [aɪm]	ich bin; ich heiße	Hello, ~ Vanessa.
	how [haʊ]	wie?	
	are [ɑ:]	bist; seid; sind	
	you [jʊ/ju:]	du; ihr; Sie	
	how are you? [haʊ ɑ: ju:]	wie geht es Ihnen/dir?	Hello Helen, ~?

	fine [faɪn]	fein; gut	
	I'm fine [aɪm faɪn]	mir geht es gut	How are you? – ~, thanks.
	thanks [θæŋks]	danke	I'm fine, ~.
	and [ənd/ænd]	und	Helen ~ Vanessa.
	this [ðɪs]	dies; das	
	is [ɪz]	ist	
	this is [ðɪs ɪz]	dies ist	Mark, ~ Helen.
	nice [naɪs]	nett; schön	
	meet [mi:t]	kennenlernen; treffen; begegnen	
	nice to meet you [naɪs tə mi:t jʊ]	angenehm; nett Sie/dich kennenzulernen	I'm Tina. – ~, Tina.
H	crossword ['krɒswɜ:d]	Kreuzworträtsel	

UNIT 1 *Step 2*

	come in [kʌm 'ɪn]	kommen Sie / komm herein	~, please.
	please [pli:z]	bitte	
S	**a** [ə]	ein/eine	
	cup [kʌp]	Tasse	
	of [əv/ɒv]	von	
	tea [ti:]	Tee	
	a cup of tea [ə kʌp əv ti:]	eine Tasse Tee	Mark, ~?
	coffee ['kɒfɪ]	Kaffee	
	an [ən]	ein/eine	
	orange ['ɒrɪndʒ]	Orange; Apfelsine	
	apple ['æpl]	Apfel	
	banana [bə'nɑ:nə]	Banane	
	biscuit ['bɪskɪt]	Plätzchen; Keks	
	ice-cream [aɪs'kri:m]	(Speise-)Eis	
D	**have** [hæv]	haben	
	seat [si:t]	(Sitz-)Platz; Sitz	
	have a seat [hæv ə si:t]	setzen Sie sich; setz dich	Come in and ~.
	thank you ['θæŋk jʊ]	danke (schön)	Have a seat. – ~.
	yes [jes]	ja	A biscuit? – ~, please.
	no [nəʊ]	nein	A sandwich? – ~, thank you.
	mum [mʌm]	Mutti; Mama; Mami	
	must [məst/mʌst]	müssen	
	be [bi:]	sein	
	you must be [ju: məst bi:]	Sie müssen / du mußt … sein	Hello, ~ Helen.
	welcome to ['welkəm tə]	willkommen in	~ London, Mark.
A	town [taʊn]	Stadt	

UNIT 1 *Step 3*

D	**where?** [weə]	wo?	~ is Tina?
	where are you from? ['weərə ju: frɒm]	wo sind Sie / bist du her?; woher sind Sie / bist du?	
	in [ɪn]	in	Krefeld is ~ Germany.
	Germany ['dʒɜ:mənɪ]	Deutschland	
	from [frəm/frɒm]	aus; von	I'm ~ Berlin and Mark is ~ Hamburg.
	not [nɒt]	nicht	I'm ~ from Berlin. I'm from Leipzig.

	he [hɪ/hiː]	er	Where is Mark from? – ~ is from Hamburg.
	's (= is) [z]	ist	Where is Norman from? – He~ from Wales.
	she [ʃɪ/ʃiː]	sie	Where is Helen from? – ~ is from Liverpool.
	too [tuː]	auch	Norman is from Cardiff and I'm from Cardiff, ~.
	isn't (= is not) [ɪznt]	ist nicht	
	but [bət/bʌt]	aber; sondern	I'm from Wales ~ Mark is from Germany.
	here [hɪə]	hier	
	the [ðə]	der; die; das	~ key is here.
	key [kiː]	Schlüssel	
	for [fə/fɔː]	für	Thank you ~ the coffee.
	number ['nʌmbə]	(Haus-)Nummer; Zahl	
	you're welcome [jɔː 'welkəm]	bitte sehr; nichts zu danken; gerne geschehen	Thank you for the coffee. – ~.
	phone [fəʊn]	Telefon	
A	introduce [ɪntrə'djuːs]	stellen Sie vor	
	your [jɔː]	dein; ihr; Ihr	
	Austria ['ɒstrɪə]	Österreich	
	Switzerland ['swɪtsələnd]	die Schweiz	
	game [geɪm]	Spiel	
	memory game ['memərɪ geɪm]	Gedächtnisspiel	
	what? [wɒt]	was?	
	what's your phone number? [wɒts jɔː fəʊn 'nʌmbə]	wie ist Deine/Ihre Telefonnummer?	
	it [ɪt]	es; sie; er	What's your phone number? – ~ is 786 527.
	ok [əʊ keɪ]	OK; in Ordnung	
	or [ɔː]	oder	
G	**aren't (= are not)** [ɑːnt]	sind nicht	
H	castle ['kɑːsl]	Schloß; Burg	

UNIT 1 *Revision and extension*

5	class [klɑːs]	Kurs; Klasse	
	list [lɪst]	Liste	
	name [neɪm]	Name	Is your ~ John? – Yes, it is. I'm John.
7	memory check ['memərɪ ˌtʃek]	Gedächtnisübung	
8	daddy ['dædɪ]	Vati; Papa; Papi	
	teenager ['tiːneɪdʒə]	Teenager	
	happy ['hæpɪ]	glücklich; froh	
	my [maɪ]	mein/meine	
	day [deɪ]	Tag	
	have a nice day [hæv ə naɪs deɪ]	viel Spaß; schönen Tag noch	
	so long [səʊ lɒŋ]	tschüs; bis bald	
U	**excuse me** [ɪk'skjuːz miː]	entschuldigen Sie / entschuldige/ entschuldigt bitte	
	can [kən/kæn]	können/kann/kannst	
	help [help]	helfen	
	me [mɪ/miː]	mich; mir	

can you help me, please? [kən ju: help mı pli:z]	können Sie / kannst du mir bitte helfen?	
what's … in English? [wɒts … ın 'ıŋglıʃ]	was bedeutet … auf englisch?	
can you repeat that, please? [kən ju: rı'pi:t ðæt pli:z]	können Sie / kannst Du das bitte wiederholen?	
of course [əv 'kɔ:s]	natürlich; selbstverständlich	

UNIT 2

I settling in ['setlıŋ ın]	sich einleben	

UNIT 2 *Step 1*

house [haʊs]	Haus	
S **cat** [kæt]	Katze	
dog [dɒg]	Hund	
photo ['fəʊtəʊ]	Foto	
television ['telıvıʒn]	Fernsehgerät; Fernseher	
cassette recorder [kə'set rı'kɔ:də]	Kassettenrecorder	
dictionary [dık'ʃənrı]	Wörterbuch	
D **have got** [həv/hæv gɒt]	haben	Mark and Tina ~ a video.
they [ðeı]	sie	Where are Karen and Paul? – ~ are in Austria.
English ['ıŋglıʃ]	englisch	~ tea is nice.
cassette [kə'set]	Kassette	
look [lʊk]	schauen Sie/schau	~, they've got a video.
really ['rıəlı]	wirklich; tatsächlich	They've got a photo of Leipzig. – ~?
problem ['prɒbləm]	Problem	
my [maı]	mein/meine	
video camera ['vıdıəʊ 'kæmrə]	Videokamera	
never mind ['nevə maınd]	es macht nichts	I haven't got my English cassettes. – ~.
camera ['kæmrə]	Kamera; Photoapparat	
good [gʊd]	gut	Your English is ~.
we [wı/wi:]	wir	Mark and I have got 2 English cassettes, but ~ haven't got a cassette recorder.
German ['dʒɜ:mən]	deutsch	~ coffee is good.
A **Mr** ['mıstə]	Herr *(vor Namen)*	~ Wilson.
G **telephone** ['telıfəʊn]	Telefon	
Mrs ['mısız]	Frau *(vor Namen)*	~ Brent.

UNIT 2 *Step 2*

family ['fæməlı]	Familie, Verwandtschaft	
friend [frend]	Freund/Freundin; Bekannter/Bekannte	
S **father** ['fɑ:ðə]	Vater	
mother ['mʌðə]	Mutter	

	husband ['hʌzbənd]	Ehemann	
	wife [waɪf]	Ehefrau	
	son [sʌn]	Sohn	
	daughter ['dɔ:tə]	Tochter	
	brother ['brʌðə]	Bruder	
	sister ['sɪstə]	Schwester	
D	**who?** [hu:]	wer?	~'s this? – It's my brother.
	his [hɪz]	sein/seine	Where's Mark? I've got ~ key.
	her [hɜ:]	ihr/ihre	Where's Tina? I've got ~ camera.
	hat [hæt]	Hut	
	awful ['ɔ:fl]	schrecklich; furchtbar	Ugh! Her hat's ~.
	student ['stju:dənt]	Student/Studentin	
A	**person** ['pɜ:sn]	Person	
	what's his name? [wɒts hɪz neɪm]	wie heißt er?; wie ist sein Name?	~? – It's Norman.
	summer ['sʌmə]	Sommer	
	conversation [kɒnvə'seɪʃn]	Gespräch	
G	**America** [ə'merɪkə]	Amerika	
	on the phone [ɒn ðə fəʊn]	am Telefon; am Apparat	Who's ~? It's John.

UNIT 2 *Step 3*

	shop [ʃɒp]	Laden; Geschäft	
	place [pleɪs]	Ort; Platz	Cambridge is a nice ~.
S	**museum** [mju:'zɪəm]	Museum	
	restaurant ['restrɒnt]	Restaurant	
	pub [pʌb]	Gaststätte; Kneipe; Wirtschaft; Lokal	
	disco ['dɪskəʊ]	Disco	
D	**hairdryer** ['heədraɪə]	Fön; Haartrockner	
	ask [ɑ:sk]	fragen	Where's my dictionary? – ~ Karen and Paul.
	's got/has got [həz/hæz gɒt]	hat	Helen ~ a daughter.
	what's … like? [wɒts … laɪk]	wie ist …?	~ London ~? – It's nice.
	a lot of [ə lɒt əv]	viel/viele; eine Menge	London has got ~ museums.
	very ['verɪ]	sehr	Her English is ~ good.
	interesting ['ɪntrəstɪŋ]	interessant	
	near [nɪə]	in der Nähe von	King's Lynn is ~ Cambridge.
	let's [lets]	laß/laßt uns	
	drink [drɪŋk]	Getränk	
	have a drink [hæv ə drɪŋk]	etwas trinken	Let's ~.
	idea [aɪ'dɪə]	Idee	
	go [gəʊ]	gehen; fahren	
	to [tʊ/tu:]	zu	
	goodbye [gʊd'baɪ]	auf Wiedersehen	
G	city ['sɪtɪ]	Stadt; Großstadt	
H	**bed-and-breakfast** [bedn'brekfəst]	Frühstückspension; Übernachtung mit Frühstück	
	now [naʊ]	jetzt; nun	We're from England but ~ we're in Germany.
	odd man out [ɒd mæn aʊt]	Außenseiter	

UNIT 2 *Revision and extension*

S	**swimming pool** ['swɪmɪŋ pu:l]	Schwimmbad; Schwimmbecken
1	pullover ['pʊləʊvə]	Pullover
	film [fɪlm]	Film
	book [bʊk]	Buch
5	super ['su:pə]	super; klasse
6	queen [kwi:n]	Königin
	prince [prɪns]	Prinz
	princess [prɪn'ses]	Prinzessin
9	girlfriend ['gɜ:lfrend]	Freundin
	hobby ['hɒbɪ]	Hobby
	write [raɪt]	schreiben
	postcard ['pəʊstkɑ:d]	Postkarte
	dear [dɪə]	Lieber/Liebe; Sehr geehrter/geehrte
U	**sorry** ['sɒrɪ]	Entschuldigung; Verzeihung; es tut mir leid
	that [ðət]	das
	that's alright [ðæts ɔ:l'raɪt]	schon gut; das macht nichts
	wrong number [rɒŋ 'nʌmbə]	falsch verbunden
	I don't understand [aɪ dəʊnt ʌndə'stænd]	ich verstehe nicht
	can you write that on the board? [kən ju: raɪt ðæt ɒn ðə bɔ:d]	kannst du / können Sie das an die Tafel schreiben?

EXTRA 1

take off ['teɪk ɒf]	Start
favourite ['feɪvrɪt]	Lieblings-
he's on flight [hi:z ɒn flaɪt]	er fliegt mit dem Flug
only ['əʊnlɪ]	nur
hour ['aʊə]	Stunde
away from [ə'weɪ frəm]	weg von
good morning [gʊd 'mɔ:nɪŋ]	guten Morgen
darling ['dɑ:lɪŋ]	Liebling; Schatz
on the line [ɒn ðə laɪn]	am Apparat
the sky above [ðə skaɪ ə'bʌv]	der Himmel über uns
blue [blu:]	blau
love [lʌv]	lieben
mystery word ['mɪstərɪ wɜ:d]	Geheimwort
radio ['reɪdɪəʊ]	Radio; Rundfunk
stereo set ['sterɪəʊ set]	Stereoanlage
famous ['feɪməs]	berühmt
street [stri:t]	Straße
home [həʊm]	Haus; Heim; Zuhause
British ['brɪtɪʃ]	britisch
Prime Minister [praɪ'mɪnɪstə]	Premierminister
often [ɒfn]	oft
on television [ɒn 'telɪvɪʒn]	im Fernsehen
with [wɪð]	mit

bobbies ['bɒbɪz]	Polizisten	
policemen [pə'li:smən]	Polizisten	
so [səʊ]	so	
minister ['mɪnɪstə]	Minister	
how many? [haʊ 'menɪ]	wie viele?	
see [si:]	sehen	
win [wɪn]	gewinnen	

UNIT 3

I getting about ['getɪŋ ə'baʊt]	herumkommen	

UNIT 3 *Step 1*

at [ət/æt]	an; in; auf	Where's John? He's ~ the pub.
at the shop [ət ðə ʃɒp]	im Laden	
D **happy** ['hæpɪ]	glücklich; froh	
nearest ['nɪərɪst]	nächster/nächste/nächstes	The ~ shop is in Bridge Street.
street [stri:t]	Straße	
along [ə'lɒŋ]	entlang	
go along [gəʊ ə'lɒŋ]	weitergehen	You ~ Castle Street.
left [left]	links	
on the left [ɒn ðə left]	links; auf der linken Seite	Go along Castle Street and it's ~.
map [mæp]	Stadtplan; Landkarte	
shopkeeper ['ʃɒpki:pə]	Ladeninhaber	
much [mʌtʃ]	viel	
how much? [haʊ mʌtʃ]	wie viel?	
how much is/are ...? [haʊ mʌtʃ ɪz/ɑ:]	wie viel kostet/kosten?	~ the dictionary? – It's £6.99.
postcard ['pəʊstkɑ:d]	Postkarte	
stamp [stæmp]	Briefmarke	
post office ['pəʊstɒfɪs]	Postamt	
turn [tɜ:n]	(ein-/ab-)biegen; drehen; wenden	
right [raɪt]	rechts	
turn right [tɜ:n raɪt]	biegen Sie/bieg rechts ein	Where's the bank? – Go along Park Street and ~.
opposite ['ɒpəzɪt]	gegenüber	The museum is ~ the park.
next to [nekst tə]	neben	The restaurant is ~ the post office.
all [ɔ:l]	alles	
is that all? [ɪz ðæt ɔ:l]	ist das alles?; sonst noch etwas?	
work [wɜ:k]	arbeiten	
A close your book [kləʊz jɔ: bʊk]	schließen Sie Ihr Buch	
G **American** [ə'merɪkən]	Amerikaner/Amerikanerin; amerikanisch	
pound [paʊnd]	Pfund	pound = £
road [rəʊd]	Straße	
H **thank you very much** [θæŋk jʊ verɪ 'mʌtʃ]	vielen herzlichen Dank	

VOCABULARY

UNIT 3 *Step 2*

S	**food** [fu:d]	Essen	
	know [nəʊ]	kennen, wissen	
D	**beer** [bɪə]	Bier	
	cheers [tʃɪəz]	Prost; zum Wohl	
	like [laɪk]	mögen; gern haben	
	do you like it? [dʊ ju: laɪk ɪt]	mögen Sie es?	
	drink [drɪŋk]	trinken	I ~ a lot of tea.
	eat [i:t]	essen	We ~ a lot of steak.
	fish and chips [fɪʃn 'tʃɪps]	Fisch und Pommes frites	
	coke [kəʊk]	Coca Cola	
	work [wɜ:k]	arbeiten	I ~ a lot.
	firm [fɜ:m]	Firma	
	state [steɪt]	Staat; staatlich	
	railway(s) ['reɪlweɪz]	Eisenbahn(en)	
	what time is it? [wɒt taɪm ɪz ɪt]	wie spät ist es?; wieviel Uhr ist es?	~? – It's 5.45.
	o'clock: it's 3 ~ [ə'klɒk]	Uhr; es ist 3 Uhr	What time is it? – It's 3 ~.
	close [kləʊz]	zumachen; schließen	
	afternoon [ɑ:ftə'nu:n]	Nachmittag	
	in the afternoon [ɪn ðɪ ɑ:ftə'nu:n]	am Nachmittag; nachmittags	A lot of restaurants close ~.
	a lot of pubs do [ə lɒt əv pʌbz dʊ]	viele Gaststätten tun es (d.h. schließen)	
A	**home** [həʊm]	Haus; Heim; Zuhause	
	at home [ət həʊm]	zu Hause	I work ~.
	pen [pen]	Stift; Füller	
G	**whisky** ['wɪskɪ]	Whisky	
	them [ðem]	sie; ihnen	
H	**morning** ['mɔ:nɪŋ]	Morgen	
	in the morning [ɪn ðə 'mɔ:nɪŋ]	am Morgen; morgens	It's 7 o'clock ~.
	evening ['i:vnɪŋ]	Abend	
	in the evening [ɪn ðɪ i:vnɪŋ]	am Abend	I go to the pub ~.
	closing time ['kləʊzɪŋ taɪm]	Schlußzeit	

UNIT 3 *Step 3*

	game [geɪm]	Spiel	
S	**at 11 (o'clock)** [ət ɪ'levn]	um 11 (Uhr)	
	sport [spɔ:t]	Sport; Sportart	
	international [ɪntə'næʃnəl]	international	
D	**play** [pleɪ]	spielen	I ~ tennis in the morning.
	why? [waɪ]	warum?	~ do you play tennis? – It's a good game.
	new [nju:]	neu	Look, this is my ~ cassette recorder.
	sports centre [spɔ:ts 'sentə]	Sportzentrum	
	exciting [ɪk'saɪtɪŋ]	aufregend	Tennis is an ~ game.
	so [səʊ]	also	I don't like beer ~ I don't drink it.
	partner ['pɑ:tnə]	Partner	
	when? [wen]	wann?	~ do you play squash? In the evening?
	usually ['ju:ʒəlɪ]	gewöhnlich; normalerweise	I ~ drink beer in the pub, not at home.

	weekend [wiːk'end]	Wochenende	We usually play tennis at the ~.
	on Saturday [ɒn]	am Samstag; samstags	I go to the sports centre ~.
	time [taɪm]	Zeit	Have you got ~ for a cup of coffee?
	have a game [hæv ə geɪm]	spielen; ein Spiel machen	Let's ~ of tennis on Saturday.
	great [greɪt]	prima; klasse; großartig	Let's go to the museum at the weekend. – That's a ~ idea.
A	**day** [deɪ]	Tag	
	week [wiːk]	Woche	
	Monday ['mʌndɪ]	Montag	
	Tuesday ['tjuːzdɪ]	Dienstag	
	Wednesday ['wenzdɪ]	Mittwoch	
	Thursday ['θɜːzdɪ]	Donnerstag	
	Friday ['fraɪdɪ]	Freitag	
	Saturday ['sætədɪ]	Samstag	
	Sunday ['sʌndɪ]	Sonntag	

UNIT 3 *Revision and extension*

2	gin [dʒɪn]	Gin	
3	pizzeria [pɪzə'rɪə]	Pizzeria	
	delicatessen [delɪkə'tesn]	Feinkostgeschäft	
	supermarket ['suːpəmɑːkɪt]	Supermarkt	
7	open ['əʊpən]	öffnen; aufmachen	
	between [bɪ'twiːn]	zwischen	
	still [stɪl]	(immer) noch	
	then [ðen]	dann	
	again [ə'gen]	wieder; noch einmal	
	also ['ɔːlsəʊ]	auch	
	all day [ɔːl deɪ]	den ganzen Tag	
	corner shop ['kɔːnə ʃɒp]	Tante-Emma-Laden	
	all week [ɔːl wiːk]	die ganze Woche	
	owner ['əʊnə]	Inhaber/Inhaberin	
	immigrant ['ɪmɪgrənt]	Einwanderer	
U	**think** [θɪŋk]	denken; glauben	I ~ the nearest bank is in Bridge Street.
	know [nəʊ]	wissen; kennen	
	I don't know [aɪ dəʊnt nəʊ]	ich weiß es nicht	When do the shops close here? – I'm sorry, ~.
	I'm a stranger here [aɪm ə 'streɪndʒə hɪə]	ich bin hier fremd; ich bin nicht von hier	Excuse me, where's the Castle Hotel? – Sorry, ~.

UNIT 4

I	people ['piːpl]	Leute; Menschen	
	plan [plæn]	Plan	

UNIT 4 *Step 1*

	neighbour ['neɪbə]	Nachbar	
S	**language** ['læŋwɪdʒ]	Sprache	

	dialect ['daɪəlekt]	Dialekt	
	speak [spi:k]	sprechen	We can ~ two languages, English and German.
	a bit of [ə bɪt əv]	ein bißchen; etwas	I usually eat ~ ice-cream in the evening.
D	does: ~ he write? [dəz hi: raɪt]	schreibt er?	
	often [ɒfn]	oft	Mr and Mrs Brent ~ go to London.
	write [raɪt]	schreiben	
	live [lɪv]	wohnen; leben	I'm American but I ~ in Switzerland.
	with [wɪð]	mit	I often play tennis ~ my brother.
	Japanese [dʒæpə'ni:z]	japanisch	
	their [ðeə]	ihr	This is Mr and Mrs Wilson and this is ~ son Terry.
	flying doctor ['flaɪɪŋ 'dɒktə]	fliegender Arzt	
	weather ['weðə]	Wetter	
	our ['aʊə]	unser/unsere	We work for Wessex Bank but ~ daughter works for the post office.
	next [nekst]	nächster/nächste/nächstes	Our ~ English class is on Tuesday.
	holiday ['hɒlədɪ]	Urlaub; Ferien	
	winter ['wɪntə]	Winter	
A	**say** [seɪ]	sagen	When I don't understand, I often ~ "Can you repeat that, please?"
G	**read** [ri:d]	lesen	We often ~ English books.
H	**on holiday** [ɒn 'hɒlədɪ]	im Urlaub	They are ~ in Austria.

UNIT 4 *Step 2*

	small talk ['smɔ:l tɔ:k]	Small Talk; Plauderei	
S	every ['evrɪ]	jeder/jede/jedes	
	bed [bed]	Bett	
	for breakfast [fə 'brekfəst]	zum Frühstück	We usually eat cornflakes ~.
	start [stɑ:t]	anfangen; beginnen	
	start work [stɑ:t wɜ:k]	zu arbeiten anfangen	Do you ~ at 8.30?
	get up [get ʌp]	aufstehen	I ~ at 10.30 at the weekend.
	newspaper ['nju:zpeɪpə]	Zeitung	
	come [kʌm]	kommen	
	come home [kʌm həʊm]	nach Hause kommen	I start work at 9 and ~ at 6.
D	**late** [leɪt]	spät	It's 11 o'clock in the evening. It's very ~.
	always ['ɔ:lweɪz]	immer	Paul ~ gets up late on Saturday.
	early ['ɜ:lɪ]	früh	It's 6 o'clock in the morning. It's ~.
	Swedish ['swi:dɪʃ]	schwedisch	
	radio station ['reɪdɪəʊ steɪʃn]	Rundfunkstation	
	news [nju:z]	Nachrichten	
	sometimes ['sʌmtaɪmz]	manchmal	We ~ go on holiday in winter.
	tired ['taɪəd]	müde	I'm very ~. Let's go to bed early.
A	**never** ['nevə]	nie	My husband always drinks tea, but I ~ drink it.

	positive ['pɒzətɪv]	positiv, bejahend	
	negative ['negətɪv]	negativ, verneinend	
	toast [təʊst]	Toast	
H	ice-hockey ['aɪshɒkɪ]	Eishockey	

UNIT 4 *Step 3*

	tourist information (office) ['tʊərɪst ɪnfə'meɪʃn 'ɒfɪs]	Fremdenverkehrsbüro	
S	remember [rɪ'membə]	sich erinnern	
	coach [kəʊtʃ]	Reisebus	
	plane [pleɪn]	Flugzeug	
	bike [baɪk]	Fahrrad	
	train [treɪn]	Zug	
	car [kɑ:]	Auto	
D	**would like ('d like)** [wʊd laɪk]	möchten	Where ~ you ~ to go? – I ~ to go to London.
	well [wel]	nun (ja); also	
	transport ['trænspɔ:t]	Transport, Verkehr	
	by (train) [baɪ treɪn]	mit (dem Zug)	They always go on holiday ~.
	open ['əʊpən]	öffnen; aufmachen	The shops usually ~ at 9 o'clock.
	tourist ['tʊərɪst]	Tourist	
	office ['ɒfɪs]	Büro	
	clerk [klɑ:k]	Angestellter	
	moment ['məʊmənt]	Moment; Augenblick	When does the museum open? – One ~, please.
	first [fɜ:st]	erster/erste/erstes	
	leave [li:v]	abfahren; abfliegen; verlassen	When does the train ~?
	too [tu:]	zu	The train leaves at 9. – Oh, that's ~ late.
	what time? [wɒt taɪm]	um wieviel Uhr?; wann?	~ do you get up?
	arrive [ə'raɪv]	ankommen	The planes to England sometimes ~ early.
A	**bus** [bʌs]	Bus	
	walk [wɔ:k]	laufen; zu Fuß gehen	I don't go to work by car. I ~.
	see [si:]	sehen; besichtigen	What would you like to ~ in Cambridge?
	there [ðeə]	da; dort	
H	station ['steɪʃn]	Bahnhof	

UNIT 4 *Revision and extension*

1	badminton ['bædmɪntən]	Badminton	
4	college ['kɒlɪdʒ]	Kolleg (= Schulform)	
	teacher ['ti:tʃə]	Lehrer/Lehrerin	
	manager ['mænədʒə]	Manager; Geschäftsführer	
	have breakfast [hæv 'brekfəst]	frühstücken	I often ~ at 8 o'clock.
	before [bɪ'fɔ:]	bevor	I often read a book ~ I go to bed.
	again [ə'gen]	wieder; noch einmal	
5	typical ['tɪpɪkl]	typisch	

6	boyfriend ['bɔɪfrend]	Freund	
9	medical centre ['medɪkl 'sentə]	medizinisches Versorgungszentrum	
	patient ['peɪʃnt]	Patient/Patientin	
	fly out; flies [flaɪ aʊt]	hinfliegen; fliegt	
	outback ['aʊtbæk]	Busch; Wüste	
	mile [maɪl]	Meile	
	emergency [ɪ'mɜ:dʒənsɪ]	Notfall	
	operate on ['ɒpəreɪt ɒn]	operieren	
	hospital ['hɒspɪtl]	Krankenhaus	
	hard [hɑ:d]	hart; schwer	
	job [dʒɒb]	Stelle; Arbeit; Beruf	
U	**get** [get]	*hier:* (hin)kommen	
	aborigine [æbə'rɪdʒənɪ]	australischer Ureinwohner	
	mean [mi:n]	bedeuten	
	put [pʊt]	tun; stellen; setzen; legen	Where can I ~ my book?
	word [wɜ:d]	Wort	
	sentence ['sentəns]	Satz	

EXTRA 2

men [men]	Männer
both [bəʊθ]	beide
man [mæn]	Mann
other ['ʌðə]	anderer/andere/anderes
on time [ɒn taɪm]	pünktlich
sun [sʌn]	Sonne
rain [reɪn]	Regen
boss [bɒs]	Chef
try [traɪ]	versuchen
rock [rɒk]	Fels
national park ['næʃnl pɑ:k]	Nationalpark
kilometre [kɪ'lɒmɪtə]	Kilometer
mountain ['maʊntɪn]	Berg
part [pɑ:t]	Teil
red [red]	rot
sand [sænd]	Sand
vegetation [vedʒɪ'teɪʃn]	Vegetation
because [bɪ'kɒz]	weil
face [feɪs]	Gesicht
there are [ðeə ɑ:]	es gibt
symbol ['sɪmbl]	Symbol
painting ['peɪntɪŋ]	Bild; Gemälde
tell [tel]	erzählen; sagen
us [ʌs]	uns
about [ə'baʊt]	über
big [bɪg]	groß
attraction [ə'trækʃn]	Attraktion
on the way [ɒn ðə weɪ]	auf dem Weg
camel ['kæml]	Kamel
farm [fɑ:m]	Bauernhof; Farm
go on a safari [gəʊ ɒn ə sə'fɑ:rɪ]	eine Safari machen

middle ['mɪdl]	Mitte	
smile [smaɪl]	lächeln	
woman ['wʊmən]	Frau	

UNIT 5

I sightseeing ['saɪtˌsiːɪŋ]	Besichtigungen	
river ['rɪvə]	Fluß	
university [juːnɪ'vɜːsətɪ]	Universität	

UNIT 5 *Step 1*

S **was** [wɒs]	war	What ~ your day like?
yesterday ['jestədɪ]	gestern	
were [wɜː]	warst; wart; waren	John and Cliff ~ in Cardiff yesterday.
D Czech [tʃek]	tschechisch	
all day [ɔːl deɪ]	den ganzen Tag	I was at home ~ yesterday.
meal [miːl]	Mahlzeit; Essen	
have a meal [hæv ə miːl]	etwas essen	I'd like to ~ in a restaurant on Sunday.
had [hæd]	hatte; hatten; hattet; hattest	We ~ a nice meal in the new Japanese restaurant on Saturday.
well [wel]	gesund	
wasn't very well ['wɒznt 'verɪ wel]	fühlte sich nicht gut	My daughter ~, so she was in bed.
punt [pʌnt]	Stocherkahn	
on [ɒn]	auf	Where's the dog? – it's ~ the bed.
a kind of [ə kaɪnd əv]	eine Art; so etwas wie	A punt is ~ boat.
boat [bəʊt]	Boot	
suddenly ['sʌdnlɪ]	plötzlich	I was at the supermarket with my son and ~ he wasn't there.
water ['wɔːtə]	Wasser	I like ~ with my meals.
A detective [dɪ'tektɪv]	Detektiv	
Royal Family ['rɔɪəl 'fæməlɪ]	Königliche Familie	
organise ['ɔːgənaɪz]	organisieren	
party ['pɑːtɪ]	Party; Fest; Feier	
guest [gest]	Gast	
right [raɪt]	richtig	
G music ['mjuːzɪk]	Musik	
last [lɑːst]	letzter/letzte/letztes	We were in Australia ~ summer.
night [naɪt]	Nacht	
last night [lɑːst naɪt]	letzte Nacht; gestern abend	Where were you ~ at 11.30?
H story ['stɔːrɪ]	Geschichte	

UNIT 5 *Step 2*

year [jɪə]	Jahr	
T July [dʒʊ'laɪ]	Juli	

	dear [dɪə]	lieber/liebe	~ Karen, Thank you very much for the postcard …
	letter [ˈletə]	Brief	
	ask (about) [ɑːsk əˈbaʊt]	fragen (nach); sich erkundigen (nach)	I'd like to ~ my teacher ~ her family.
	stay [steɪ]	bleiben; übernachten	I often ~ at a hotel when I'm on holiday.
	then [ðen]	dann	I had an apple and ~ I had a cup of tea.
	hire [ˈhaɪə]	mieten; leihen	I haven't got a car, so I always ~ one on holiday.
	visit [ˈvɪzɪt]	besuchen	We often ~ my mother at the weekend.
	camp [kæmp]	zelten	I never stay at a hotel. I always ~.
	lake [leɪk]	See	
	rain [reɪn]	regnen; Regen	It doesn't ~ very much in Alice Springs.
	travel [ˈtrævl]	reisen; fahren	They always ~ to London by coach.
	enjoy [ɪnˈdʒɔɪ]	genießen	
	did [dɪd]	(Vergangenheit von *do*)	~ you enjoy your day in Cambridge?
	do [duː]	tun; machen	What did you ~ last night? – I visited my girlfriend.
	love [lʌv]	viele Grüße; liebe Grüße	… enjoy your holiday. ~ Peter.
G	August [ˈɔːgəst]	August	
	second [ˈsekənd]	zweiter/zweite/zweites	
H	folk museum [ˈfəʊk mjuːˈzɪəm]	Heimatmuseum	

UNIT 5 *Step 3*

S	**went** [went]	ging(en/-est/-et); fuhr(en/-st/-t)	Mark ~ to Liverpool yesterday.
	tour [tʊə]	Tour; Rundfahrt; Rundreise	
	go on a tour [gəʊ ɒn ə tʊə]	eine Tour/Rundfahrt machen	Tourists often ~ of London by bus.
	saw [sɔː]	sah(en/-st/-t)	I ~ Janet last Monday.
	came [keɪm]	kam(en/-st/-t)	We ~ home late last night.
D	**everything** [ˈevrɪθɪŋ]	alles	
	lunch [lʌntʃ]	Mittagessen	
	have lunch [hæv lʌntʃ]	zu Mittag essen	I usually ~ at 12 o'clock.
	lovely [ˈlʌvlɪ]	schön; herrlich; wunderschön	Her house is very nice. It's ~.
	long [lɒŋ]	lang	
	around: travel ~ [əˈraʊnd]	herumreisen	We ~ all day.
	hour [ˈaʊə]	Stunde	I worked for an ~ on Saturday morning.
A	**café** [ˈkæfeɪ]	Café	
	skateboard [ˈskeɪtbɔːd]	Skateboard	
	school [skuːl]	Schule	
	at school [ət skuːl]	in der Schule	She reads a lot of books ~.
G	**cinema** [ˈsɪnəmə]	Kino	
	who … with? [huː wɪð]	mit wem?	~ did you go to London ~? – I went with my sister.

H	diary ['daɪərɪ]	Tagebuch; Kalender	
	club [klʌb]	Club; Verein	
	on TV [ɒn tiː viː]	im Fernsehen	

UNIT 5 *Revision and extension*

1	opposite ['ɒpəzɪt]	Gegenteil	
6	sweet [swiːt]	süß	
8	old [əʊld]	alt	
	beautiful ['bjuːtɪfʊl]	schön	
	market place ['mɑːkɪt pleɪs]	Marktplatz	
	modern ['mɒdən]	modern	
	shopping centre ['ʃɒpɪŋ 'sentə]	Einkaufszentrum	
	famous ['feɪməs]	berühmt	
	citizen ['sɪtɪzən]	Bürger/Bürgerin	
	found [faʊnd]	gründen	
	football ['fʊtbɔːl]	Fußball	
	gardens ['gɑːdnz]	Gartenanlagen	
	there is [ðeə ɪz]	es gibt; da ist	
	festival ['festɪvl]	Festival; Fest	
U	**tell** [tel]	erzählen; sagen	
	ago: … years ago [ə'gəʊ]	vor: vor … Jahren	
	I can't remember [aɪ kɑːnt rɪ'membə]	ich kann mich nicht erinnern	

UNIT 6

I	**sea: by the ~** [siː]	Meer: am Meer	
	beach [biːtʃ]	Strand	
	village ['vɪlɪdʒ]	Dorf	
	windmill ['wɪnmɪl]	Windmühle	

UNIT 6 *Step 1*

	life history [laɪf 'hɪstrɪ]	Lebensgeschichte	
S	**was/were born** [wɒz/wɜː bɔːn]	bin/ist/sind/bist/seid geboren	My daughter ~ in 1985.
	hospital ['hɒspɪtl]	Krankenhaus	She was born in Guy's ~.
	met [met]	traf(en-st/-t); lernte(n/-st/-t) kennen; begegnete(n/-st/-t)	I ~ my husband in 1986.
	get married [get 'mærɪd]	heiraten	
	got married [gɒt 'mærɪd]	heiratete(n/-st-t)	We ~ in August.
	business ['bɪznɪs]	Firma; Betrieb	He opened a ~ last year.
D	reporter [rɪ'pɔːtə]	Reporter	
	big [bɪg]	groß	
	money ['mʌnɪ]	Geld	
	at the time [ət ðə taɪm]	zu der Zeit	I didn't work for three years. I had two small sons ~.
	full-time ['fʊl taɪm]	ganztags	I worked all day. I worked ~.
	small [smɔːl]	klein	
	train [treɪn]	eine Ausbildung machen; ausgebildet werden	She ~ed for 2 years before she started her job.

	from … to [frɒm … tʊ]	von … bis	The shops open ~ 9 o'clock ~ 5 o'clock.
	work [wɜːk]	Arbeit	I like my ~ very much.
	different ['dɪfrənt]	verschieden; unterschiedlich	
	country, -ies ['kʌntrɪ]	Land, Länder	Australia is an exciting ~.
	us [ʌs]	uns	They often visit ~ at the weekend.
	them [ðem]	sie; ihnen	She met Karen and Paul and liked ~.
A	fill in [fɪl ɪn]	ausfüllen	
	form [fɔːm]	Formular	
	talk to [tɔːk tʊ]	sprechen mit	
	notes [nəʊts]	Notizen	
	think of [θɪŋk əv]	halten von	What do you ~ your English class?
G	**old** [əʊld]	alt	How ~ are you? – I'm 26.
	bar [bɑː]	Bar	
H	booming ['buːmɪŋ]	blühend	
	profile ['prəʊfaɪl]	Kurzbiographie	
	interview ['ɪntəvjuː]	interviewen	
	active ['æktɪv]	aktiv	
	attractive [ə'træktɪv]	attraktiv	
	lady ['leɪdɪ]	Dame; Frau	
	because [bɪ'kɒz]	weil	
	from all over Europe [frəm ɔːl ˌəʊvə 'jʊərəp]	aus ganz Europa	
	smile [smaɪl]	Lächeln	
	want to [wɒnt tə]	wollen	
	at first [ət fɜːst]	zuerst	
	garage ['gærɑːʒ]	(Auto-)Werkstatt	
	mechanic [mɪ'kænɪk]	Mechaniker	
	love [lʌv]	lieben	
	good luck [gʊd lʌk]	viel Glück	

UNIT 6 *Step 2*

	picnic ['pɪknɪk]	Picknick	
S	**give** [gɪv]	geben	
	quiet ['kwaɪət]	ruhig; leise	
	crowded ['kraʊdɪd]	voll; überfüllt	
	relaxing [rɪ'læksɪŋ]	entspannend; erholsam	
D	**pass** [pɑːs]	reichen	Can you ~ me the tea, please?
	here you are [hɪə jʊ ɑː]	bitte schön	Can I have the coffee please? – ~.
	ketchup ['ketʃʌp]	Ketchup	
	have tea [hæv tiː]	Tee trinken	We often ~ in a small cafe near here.
	buy [baɪ]	kaufen	
	souvenir [suːvə'nɪə]	Souvenir	
	take [teɪk]	(mit)nehmen	
	bought [bɔːt]	kaufte(n)	What did you buy them? – I ~ them a cassette.
	black [blæk]	schwarz	
	umbrella [ʌm'brelə]	Regenschirm	

	her [hɜː]	sie; ihr	What did you buy Jane? – I bought ~ a book.
	tea cosy ['tiː kəʊzɪ]	Teewärmer	
	take a photo [teɪk ə 'fəʊtəʊ]	ein Foto machen	Can I ~ of your family, please?
	send [send]	schicken; senden	I ~ a lot of letters to Germany.
	photo album ['fəʊtəʊ 'ælbəm]	Fotoalbum	
	come on [kʌm ɒn]	komm(t) (jetzt); mach(t) schon	
	smile [smaɪl]	lächeln	When she takes a photo of me, I always ~.
A	**him** [hɪm]	ihn; ihm	Where did you meet your husband? – I met ~ in Birmingham.
	present ['preznt]	Geschenk	
	table ['teɪbl]	Tabelle	
	choose [tʃuːz]	aus(wählen)	
H	past tense [pɑːst tens]	Vergangenheitsform	

UNIT 6 *Step 3*

D	**address** [ə'dres]	Adresse	
	one day [wʌn deɪ]	eines Tages	I must visit you ~.
	spell [spel]	buchstabieren	Can you ~ that, please?
	taxi ['tæksɪ]	Taxi	
	trip [trɪp]	Reise; Ausflug	
	everyone ['evrɪwʌn]	jeder(mann); alle	I like ~ in the class.
	friendly ['frendlɪ]	freundlich	
	hope [həʊp]	hoffen	I ~ I can visit you next year.
G	letter ['letə]	Buchstabe	
	thank [θæŋk]	danken	
	card [kɑːd]	Karte	
H	receptionist [rɪ'sepʃənɪst]	Person am Empfang	
	green [griːn]	grün	
	town hall [taʊn hɔːl]	Rathaus	
	church [tʃɜːtʃ]	Kirche	
	service ['sɜːvɪs]	Bedienung	
	gaol [dʒeɪl]	Gefängnis	

UNIT 6 *Revision and extension*

2	**after** ['ɑːftə]	nach; nachdem	I always read the newspaper ~ breakfast.
4	thing [θɪŋ]	Ding	
8	tradition [trə'dɪʃn]	Tradition	
	pack [pæk]	packen; einpacken	
	basket ['bɑːskɪt]	Korb	
	lemonade [lemə'neɪd]	Limonade	
	go out [gəʊ aʊt]	(hin)ausgehen	
	into the country ['ɪntə ðə 'kʌntrɪ]	aufs Land	
	sit [sɪt]	sitzen	
	grass [grɑːs]	Gras	
	ball [bɔːl]	Ball	
	frisbee ['frɪzbiː]	Frisbee	
	cricket match ['krɪkɪt mætʃ]	Cricketspiel	

watch [wɒtʃ]	zusehen
U **have a nice day** [hæv ə naɪs deɪ]	schönen Tag
have a nice time [hæv ə naɪs taɪm]	schöne Zeit; viel Spaß

EXTRA 3

I don't mind [aɪ dəʊnt maɪnd]	es macht mir nichts aus
maybe ['meɪbi:]	vielleicht
same [seɪm]	selber/selbe/selbes
I'll be [aɪl bi:]	ich werde … sein
don't say [dəʊnt seɪ]	sag nicht
wonderful ['wʌndəfʊl]	wunderbar
most [məʊst]	die meisten
capital ['kæpɪtl]	Hauptstadt
main street [meɪn stri:t]	Hauptstraße
side [saɪd]	Seite
monument ['mɒnjʊmənt]	Monument
hill [hɪl]	Hügel
marvellous ['mɑ:vələs]	wunderbar
all over the world [ɔ:l 'əʊvə ðə wɜ:ld]	überall in der Welt
cultural ['kʌltʃərəl]	kulturell
event [ɪ'vent]	Ereignis; Veranstaltung
theatre ['θɪətə]	Theater

DICTIONARY

Hier finden Sie sämtliche Wörter und Wendungen des Buches in alphabetischer Reihenfolge. Neben der deutschen Übersetzung steht der Fundort, d.h. der Ort, wo das Wort im Buch vorkommt. Wollen Sie mehr über das Wort wissen, können Sie es mit Hilfe der Fundortangabe im *Vocabulary* nachschlagen.

Die erste Ziffer der Fundortangabe weist auf die Unit hin, in der das Wort vorkommt, die zweite (nach dem Punkt) auf den Step. 3.2 heißt also Unit 3, Step 2. Die anderen Abkürzungen bedeuten:
E = Extra
R = Revision and extension
S = Starter (am Anfang des Buches, S. 4ff.).

A

a [ə] ein/eine 1.2
aborigine [æbə'rɪdʒənɪ] australischer Ureinwohner *4R*
about [ə'baʊt] über *E2*
above [ə'bʌv] über *E1*
active ['æktɪv] aktiv *6.1*
address [ə'dres] Adresse 6.3
after ['ɑ:ftə] nach; nachdem 6R
afternoon [ɑ:ftə'nu:n] Nachmittag 3.2
again [ə'gen] wieder; noch einmal *3R*, 4R
ago [ə'gəʊ] vor 5R: **... years ago** vor ... Jahren 5R
all [ɔ:l] alles 3.1
all day [ɔ:l deɪ] den ganzen Tag *3R*, 5.1
all over the world [ɔ:l 'əʊvə ðə wɜ:ld] überall in der Welt *E3*
all week [ɔ:l wi:k] die ganze Woche *3R*
along [ə'lɒŋ] entlang 3.1
alright [ɔ:l'raɪt]: **that's alright** schon gut; das macht nichts 2R
also ['ɔ:lsəʊ] auch *3R*
always ['ɔ:lweɪz] immer 4.2
am [æm] bin 1.1
America [ə'merɪkə] Amerika 2.2
American [ə'merɪkən] Amerikaner/Amerikanerin; amerikanisch 3.1
an [ən] ein/eine 1.2
and [ənd/ænd] und 1.1
apple ['æpl] Apfel 1.2
are [ɑ:] bist; seid; sind 1.1
aren't (= are not) [ɑ:nt] sind nicht 1.3
around [ə'raʊnd]: **travel around** herumreisen 5.3
arrival [ə'raɪvl] Ankunft *1.1*
arrive [ə'raɪv] ankommen 4.3
ask [ɑ:sk] fragen 2.3
ask (about) [ɑ:sk ə'baʊt] fragen (nach); sich erkundigen (nach) 5.2
at [ət/æt] an; in; auf 3.1
at 11 (o'clock) [ət ɪ'levn] um 11 (Uhr) 3.3
at first [ət fɜ:st] zuerst *6.1*
at home [ət həʊm] zu Hause 3.2
at school [ət sku:l] in der Schule 5.3
at the shop [ət ðə ʃɒp] im Laden 3.1
at the time [ət ðə taɪm] zu der Zeit 6.1
attraction [ə'trækʃn] Attraktion *E2*
attractive [ə'træktɪv] attraktiv *6.1*
August ['ɔ:gəst] August *5.2*
Austria ['ɒstrɪə] Österreich 1.3
away from [ə'weɪ frəm] weg von *E1*
awful ['ɔ:fl] schrecklich; furchtbar 2.2

B

badminton ['bædmɪntən] Badminton *4R*
ball [bɔ:l] Ball *6R*
banana [bə'nɑ:nə] Banane 1.2
bank [bæŋk] Bank S
bar [bɑ:] Bar *6.1*
basket ['bɑ:skɪt] Korb *6R*
be [bi:] sein 1.2: **I'll be** ich werde ... sein *E3*
beach [bi:tʃ] Strand 6.1
beautiful ['bju:tɪfʊl] schön *5R*
because [bɪ'kɒz] weil *E2*, *6.1*
bed [bed] Bett 4.2
bed-and-breakfast [bedn'brekfəst] Frühstückspension; Übernachtung mit Frühstück 2.3
beer [bɪə] Bier 3.2
before [bɪ'fɔ:] bevor 4R
between [bɪ'twi:n] zwischen *3R*
big [bɪg] groß *E2*, 6.1
bike [baɪk] Fahrrad 4.3
biscuit ['bɪskɪt] Plätzchen; Keks 1.2
bit [bɪt]: **a bit of** ein bißchen; etwas 4.1
black [blæk] schwarz 6.2
blue [blu:] blau *E1*
boat [bəʊt] Boot 5.1
bobbies ['bɒbɪz] Polizisten *E1*
book [bʊk] Buch 2R
booming ['bu:mɪŋ] blühend *6.1*
boss [bɒs] Chef *E2*
both [bəʊθ] beide *E2*
bought [bɔ:t] kaufte(n) 6.2
boyfriend ['bɔɪfrend] Freund *4R*
breakfast ['brekfəst] Frühstück 2.3: **have breakfast** frühstücken 4R
British ['brɪtɪʃ] britisch *E1*
brother ['brʌðə] Bruder 2.2
bus [bʌs] Bus 4.3
business ['bɪznɪs] Firma; Betrieb 6.1
but [bət/bʌt] aber; sondern 1.3
buy [baɪ] kaufen 6.2
by (train) [baɪ treɪn] mit (dem Zug) 4.3

C

café ['kæfeɪ] Café 5.3
came [keɪm] kam(en/-st/-t) 5.3
camel ['kæml] Kamel *E2*
camera ['kæmrə] Kamera; Photoapparat 2.1
camp [kæmp] zelten 5.2
can [kən/kæn] können/kann/kannst 1R
can you help me, please? [kən ju: help mɪ pli:z] können Sie / kannst du mir bitte helfen? 1R
can you repeat that, please? [kən ju: rɪ'pi:t ðæt pli:z] können Sie / kannst Du das bitte wiederholen? 1R

can you write that on the board? [kən ju: raɪt ðæt ɒn ðə bɔ:d] kannst du / können Sie das an die Tafel schreiben? 2R
capital ['kæpɪtl] Hauptstadt *E3*
car [kɑ:] Auto 4.3
card [kɑ:d] Karte *6.3*
cassette [kə'set] Kassette 2.1
cassette recorder [kə'set rɪ'kɔ:də] Kassettenrecorder 2.1
castle ['kɑ:sl] Schloß; Burg *1.3*
cat [kæt] Katze 2.1
cheers [tʃɪəz] Prost; zum Wohl 3.2
choose [tʃu:z] aus(wählen) *6.2*
church [tʃɜ:tʃ] Kirche *6.3*
cinema ['sɪnəmə] Kino 5.3
citizen ['sɪtɪzən] Bürger/Bürgerin *5R*
city ['sɪtɪ] Stadt; Großstadt *2.3*
class [klɑ:s] Kurs; Klasse *1R*
clerk [klɑ:k] Angestellter *4.3*
close [kləʊz] zumachen; schließen 3.2
close your book [kləʊz jɔ: bʊk] schließen Sie Ihr Buch *3.1*
closing time ['kləʊzɪŋ taɪm] Schlußzeit *3.2*
club [klʌb] Club; Verein *5.3*
coach [kəʊtʃ] Reisebus *4.3*
coffee ['kɒfɪ] Kaffee 1.2
coke [kəʊk] Coca Cola 3.2
college ['kɒlɪdʒ] Kolleg (= Schulform) *4R*
come [kʌm] kommen 4.2
come home [kʌm həʊm] nach Hause kommen 4.2
come in [kʌm 'ɪn] kommen Sie / komm herein 1.2
come on [kʌm ɒn] komm(t) (jetzt); mach(t) schon *6.2*
computer [kəm'pju:tə] Computer S
conversation [kɒnvə'seɪʃn] Gespräch *2.2*
corner shop ['kɔ:nə ʃɒp] Tante-Emma-Laden *3R*
country, -ies ['kʌntrɪ] Land, Länder 6.1
cricket match ['krɪkɪt mætʃ] Cricketspiel *6R*
crossword ['krɒswɜ:d] Kreuzworträtsel *1.1*
crowded ['kraʊdɪd] voll; überfüllt *6.2*
cultural ['kʌltʃərəl] kulturell *E3*
cup [kʌp] Tasse 1.2: **a cup of tea** eine Tasse Tee 1.2
Czech [tʃek] tschechisch *5.1*

D

'd like [d laɪk] möchten 4.3
daddy ['dædɪ] Vati; Papa; Papi *1R*
darling ['dɑ:lɪŋ] Liebling; Schatz *E1*
daughter ['dɔ:tə] Tochter 2.2
day [deɪ] Tag *1R*, 3.3
dear [dɪə] Lieber/Liebe; Sehr geehrter/geehrte *2R*, 5.2
delicatessen [delɪkə'tesn] Feinkostgeschäft *3R*
detective [dɪ'tektɪv] Detektiv *5.1*
dialect ['daɪəlekt] Dialekt *4.1*
diary ['daɪərɪ] Tagebuch; Kalender *5.3*
dictionary [dɪk'ʃənrɪ] Wörterbuch 2.1
did [dɪd] (Vergangenheit von *do*) 5.2
different ['dɪfrənt] verschieden; unterschiedlich 6.1
disco ['dɪskəʊ] Disco 2.3
do [du:] tun; machen 5.2: **does he write?** schreibt er? 4.1; **don't say** sag nicht *E3*
dog [dɒg] Hund 2.1
drink [drɪŋk] Getränk 2.3: **have a drink** etwas trinken 2.3
drink [drɪŋk] trinken 3.2

E

early ['ɜ:lɪ] früh 4.2
eat [i:t] essen 3.2
emergency [ɪ'mɜ:dʒənsɪ] Notfall *4R*
English ['ɪŋglɪʃ] englisch 2.1
enjoy [ɪn'dʒɔɪ] genießen 5.2
evening ['i:vnɪŋ] Abend 3.2
event [ɪ'vent] Ereignis; Veranstaltung *E3*
every ['evrɪ] jeder/jede/jedes *4.2*
everyone ['evrɪwʌn] jeder(mann); alle 6.3
everything ['evrɪθɪŋ] alles 5.3
exciting [ɪk'saɪtɪŋ] aufregend 3.3
excuse me [ɪk'skju:z mi:] entschuldigen Sie / entschuldige/entschuldigt bitte 1R

F

face [feɪs] Gesicht *E2*
family ['fæməlɪ] Familie, Verwandtschaft 2.2
famous ['feɪməs] berühmt *E1*, *5R*
farm [fɑ:m] Bauernhof; Farm *E2*
father ['fɑ:ðə] Vater 2.2
favourite ['feɪvrɪt] Lieblings- *E1*
festival ['festɪvl] Festival; Fest *5R*
fill in [fɪl ɪn] ausfüllen *6.1*
film [fɪlm] Film 2R
fine [faɪn] fein; gut 1.1: **I'm fine** mir geht es gut 1.1
firm [fɜ:m] Firma 3.2
first [fɜ:st] erster/erste/erstes 4.3
fish and chips [fɪʃn 'tʃɪps] Fisch und Pommes frites *3.2*
flight [flaɪt] Flug *E1*
fly out; flies [flaɪ aʊt] hinfliegen; fliegt *4R*
flying doctor ['flaɪɪŋ 'dɒktə] fliegender Arzt *4.1*
folk museum ['fəʊk mju:'zɪəm] Heimatmuseum *5.2*
food [fu:d] Essen 3.2
football ['fʊtbɔ:l] Fußball *5R*
for [fə/fɔ:] für 1.3: **for breakfast** zum Frühstück 4.2
form [fɔ:m] Formular *6.1*
found [faʊnd] gründen *5R*
Friday ['fraɪdɪ] Freitag 3.3
friend [frend] Freund/Freundin; Bekannter/Bekannte 2.2
friendly ['frendlɪ] freundlich 6.3
frisbee ['frɪzbi:] Frisbee *6R*
from [frəm/frɒm] aus; von 1.3
from ... to [frɒm ... tʊ] von ... bis 6.1
from all over Europe [frəm ɔ:l ˌəʊvə 'jʊərəp] aus ganz Europa *6.1*
full-time ['fʊl taɪm] ganztags 6.1

G

game [geɪm] Spiel *1.3*, 3.3
gaol [dʒeɪl] Gefängnis *6.3*

garage ['gærɑːʒ] (Auto-)Werkstatt *6.1*
gardens ['gɑːdnz] Gartenanlagen *5R*
German ['dʒɜːmən] deutsch 2.1
Germany ['dʒɜːmənɪ] Deutschland 1.3
get [get] *hier:* (hin)kommen 4R
get married [get 'mærɪd] heiraten 6.1
get up [get ʌp] aufstehen 4.2
getting about ['getɪŋ ə'baʊt] herumkommen *3.1*
gin [dʒɪn] Gin *3R*
girlfriend ['gɜːlfrend] Freundin *2R*
give [gɪv] geben 6.2
go [gəʊ] gehen; fahren 2.3
go along [gəʊ ə'lɒŋ] weitergehen 3.1
go on a safari [gəʊ ɒn ə sə'fɑːrɪ] eine Safari machen *E2*
go on a tour [gəʊ ɒn ə tʊə] eine Tour/Rundfahrt machen 5.3
go out [gəʊ aʊt] (hin)ausgehen *6R*
golf [gɒlf] Golf S
good [gʊd] gut 2.1
good luck [gʊd lʌk] viel Glück *6.1*
good morning [gʊd 'mɔːnɪŋ] guten Morgen *E1*
goodbye [gʊd'baɪ] auf Wiedersehen 2.3
got married [gɒt 'mærɪd] heiratete(n/-st-t) 6.1
grass [grɑːs] Gras *6R*
great [greɪt] prima; klasse; großartig 3.3
green [griːn] grün *6.3*
guest [gest] Gast 5.1

H

had [hæd] hatte; hatten; hattet; hattest 5.1
hairdryer ['heədraɪə] Fön; Haartrockner 2.3
hamburger ['hæmbɜːgə] Hamburger S
happy ['hæpɪ] glücklich; froh *1R*, 3.1
hard [hɑːd] hart; schwer *4R*
has got [hæz gɒt] hat 2.3
hat [hæt] Hut 2.2
have [hæv] haben 1.2
have a drink [hæv ə drɪŋk] etwas trinken 2.3
have a game [hæv ə geɪm] spielen; ein Spiel machen 3.3
have a meal [hæv ə miːl] etwas essen 5.1
have a nice day [hæv ə naɪs deɪ] viel Spaß; schönen Tag noch *1R*, 6R
have a nice time [hæv ə naɪs taɪm] schöne Zeit; viel Spaß 6R
have a seat [hæv ə siːt] setzen Sie sich; setz dich 1.2
have breakfast [hæv 'brekfəst] frühstücken 4R
have got [həv/hæv gɒt] haben 2.1
have lunch [hæv lʌntʃ] zu Mittag essen 5.3
have tea [hæv tiː] Tee trinken 6.2
he [hɪ/hiː] er 1.3
hello [hə'ləʊ] Guten Tag; Grüß Gott; Grüezi; Hallo 1.1
help [help] helfen 1R
her [hɜː] ihr/ihre 2.2
her [hɜː] sie; ihr 6.2
here [hɪə] hier 1.3
here you are [hɪə jʊ ɑː] bitte schön 6.2
hill [hɪl] Hügel *E3*
him [hɪm] ihn; ihm 6.2
hire ['haɪə] mieten; leihen 5.2
his [hɪz] sein/seine 2.2
hobby ['hɒbɪ] Hobby *2R*
holiday ['hɒlədɪ] Urlaub; Ferien 4.1: **on holiday** im Urlaub 4.1
home [həʊm] Haus; Heim; Zuhause *E1*, 3.2: **at home** zu Hause 3.2
hope [həʊp] hoffen 6.3
hospital ['hɒspɪtl] Krankenhaus *4R*, 6.1
hotel [həʊ'tel] Hotel S
hour ['aʊə] Stunde *E1*, 5.3
house [haʊs] Haus 2.1
how [haʊ] wie? 1.1
how are you? [haʊ ɑː juː] wie geht es Ihnen/dir? 1.1
how many? [haʊ 'menɪ] wie viele? *E1*
how much? [haʊ mʌtʃ] wie viel? 3.1: **how much is/are ...?** wie viel kostet/kosten? 3.1
husband ['hʌzbənd] Ehemann 2.2

I

I [aɪ] ich 1.1
I'm [aɪm] ich bin; ich heiße 1.1
ice-cream [aɪs'kriːm] (Speise-)Eis 1.2
ice-hockey ['aɪshɒkɪ] Eishockey *4.2*
idea [aɪ'dɪə] Idee 2.3
immigrant ['ɪmɪgrənt] Einwanderer *3R*
in [ɪn] in 1.3
in the afternoon [ɪn ðɪ ɑːftə'nuːn] am Nachmittag; nachmittags 3.2
in the evening [ɪn ðɪ iːvnɪŋ] am Abend 3.2
in the morning [ɪn ðə 'mɔːnɪŋ] am Morgen; morgens 3.2
interesting ['ɪntrəstɪŋ] interessant 2.3
international [ɪntə'næʃnəl] international *3.3*
interview ['ɪntəvjuː] interviewen *6.1*
into the country ['ɪntə ðə 'kʌntrɪ] aufs Land *6R*
introduce [ɪntrə'djuːs] stellen Sie vor *1.3*
is [ɪz] ist 1.1
is that all? [ɪz ðæt ɔːl] ist das alles?; sonst noch etwas? 3.1
isn't (= is not) [ɪznt] ist nicht 1.3
it [ɪt] es; sie; er 1.3

J

Japanese [dʒæpə'niːz] japanisch *4.1*
jeans [dʒiːnz] Jeans S
job [dʒɒb] Stelle; Arbeit; Beruf 4R
July [dʒʊ'laɪ] Juli *5.2*

K

ketchup ['ketʃʌp] Ketchup *6.2*
key [kiː] Schlüssel 1.3
kilometre [kɪ'lɒmɪtə] Kilometer *E2*
kind [kaɪnd]: **a kind of** eine Art; so etwas wie 5.1

know [nəʊ] kennen, wissen *3.2*, 3R: **I don't know** ich weiß es nicht 3R

L

lady ['leɪdɪ] Dame; Frau *6.1*
lake [leɪk] See 5.2
language ['læŋwɪdʒ] Sprache 4.1
last [lɑːst] letzter/letzte/letztes 5.1
last night [lɑːst naɪt] letzte Nacht; gestern abend 5.1
late [leɪt] spät 4.2
leave [liːv] abfahren; abfliegen; verlassen 4.3
left [left] links 3.1: **on the left** links; auf der linken Seite 3.1
lemonade [lemə'neɪd] Limonade *6R*
let's [lets] laß/laßt uns 2.3
letter ['letə] Brief 5.2
letter ['letə] Buchstabe *6.3*
life history [laɪf 'hɪstrɪ] Lebensgeschichte *6.1*
like [laɪk] mögen; gern haben 3.2: **do you like it?** mögen Sie es? 3.2
like [laɪk]: **what's … like?** wie ist …? 2.3
list [lɪst] Liste *1R*
live [lɪv] wohnen; leben 4.1
long [lɒŋ] lang 5.3: **so long** tschüs; bis bald *1R*
look [lʊk] schauen Sie/schau 2.1
lot [lɒt]: **a lot of** viel/viele; eine Menge 2.3
love [lʌv] lieben *E1*, *6.1*
love [lʌv] viele Grüße; liebe Grüße 5.2
lovely ['lʌvlɪ] schön; herrlich; wunderschön 5.3
lunch [lʌntʃ] Mittagessen 5.3: **have lunch** zu Mittag essen 5.3

M

'm (= am) [m/æm] bin 1.1
main street [meɪn striːt] Hauptstraße *E3*
man [mæn] Mann *E2*
manager ['mænədʒə] Manager; Geschäftsführer 4R
map [mæp] Stadtplan; Landkarte 3.1
market place ['mɑːkɪt pleɪs] Marktplatz *5R*
married ['mærɪd]: **get married** heiraten 6.1; **got married** heiratete(n/-st/-t) 6.1
marvellous ['mɑːvələs] wunderbar *E3*
maybe ['meɪbiː] vielleicht *E3*
me [mɪ/miː] mich; mir 1R
meal [miːl] Mahlzeit; Essen 5.1: **have a meal** essen 5.1
mean [miːn] bedeuten 4R
mechanic [mɪ'kænɪk] Mechaniker *6.1*
medical centre ['medɪkl 'sentə] medizinisches Versorgungszentrum *4R*
meet [miːt] kennenlernen; treffen; begegnen 1.1
memory check ['meməri ˌtʃek] Gedächtnisübung *1R*
memory game ['meməri geɪm] Gedächtnisspiel *1.3*
men [men] Männer *E2*
met [met] traf(en-st/-t); lernte(n/-st/-t) kennen; begegnete(n/-st/-t) 6.1
middle ['mɪdl] Mitte *E2*
mile [maɪl] Meile *4R*
mind [maɪnd]: **I don't mind** es macht mir nichts aus *E3*
minister ['mɪnɪstə] Minister *E1*
modern ['mɒdən] modern *5R*
moment ['məʊmənt] Moment; Augenblick 4.3
Monday ['mʌndɪ] Montag 3.3
money ['mʌnɪ] Geld 6.1
monument ['mɒnjʊmənt] Monument *E3*
morning ['mɔːnɪŋ] Morgen 3.2
most [məʊst] die meisten *E3*
mother ['mʌðə] Mutter 2.2
mountain ['maʊntɪn] Berg *E2*
mountain bike ['maʊntɪn baɪk] Mountainbike S
Mr ['mɪstə] Herr *(vor Namen)* 2.1
Mrs ['mɪsɪz] Frau *(vor Namen)* 2.1
much [mʌtʃ] viel 3.1
mum [mʌm] Mutti; Mama; Mami 1.2
museum [mjuː'zɪəm] Museum 2.3
music ['mjuːzɪk] Musik *5.1*
must [məst/mʌst] müssen 1.2
my [maɪ] mein/meine *1R*, 2.1
mystery word ['mɪstərɪ wɜːd] Geheimwort *E1*

N

name [neɪm] Name 1R
national park ['næʃnl pɑːk] Nationalpark *E2*
near [nɪə] in der Nähe von 2.3
nearest ['nɪərɪst] nächster/nächste/nächstes 3.1
negative ['negətɪv] negativ, verneinend *4.2*
neighbour ['neɪbə] Nachbar *4.1*
never ['nevə] nie 4.2
never mind ['nevə maɪnd] es macht nichts 2.1
new [njuː] neu 3.3
news [njuːz] Nachrichten *4.2*
newspaper ['njuːzpeɪpə] Zeitung 4.2
next [nekst] nächster/nächste/nächstes 4.1
next to [nekst tə] neben 3.1
nice [naɪs] nett; schön 1.1
nice to meet you [naɪs tə miːt jʊ] angenehm; nett Sie/dich kennenzulernen 1.1
night [naɪt] Nacht 5.1
no [nəʊ] nein 1.2
not [nɒt] nicht 1.3
notes [nəʊts] Notizen *6.1*
now [naʊ] jetzt; nun 2.3
number ['nʌmbə] (Haus-)Nummer; Zahl 1.3

O

o'clock [ə'klɒk] Uhr 3.2: **it's 3 o'clock** es ist 3 Uhr 3.2
odd man out [ɒd mæn aʊt] Außenseiter *2.3*
of [əv/ɒv] von 1.2
of course [əv 'kɔːs] natürlich; selbstverständlich 1R
office ['ɒfɪs] Büro 4.3
often [ɒfn] oft *E1*, 4.1
ok [əʊ keɪ] OK; in Ordnung 1.3
old [əʊld] alt *5R*, 6.1
on [ɒn] auf 5.1
on holiday [ɒn 'hɒlədɪ] im Urlaub 4.1

on Saturday [ɒn] am Samstag; samstags 3.3
on television [ɒn ˈtelɪvɪʒn] im Fernsehen *E1*
on the left [ɒn ðə left] links; auf der linken Seite 3.1
on the line [ɒn ðə laɪn] am Apparat *E1*
on the phone [ɒn ðə fəʊn] am Telefon; am Apparat *2.2*
on the way [ɒn ðə weɪ] auf dem Weg *E2*
on time [ɒn taɪm] pünktlich *E2*
on TV [ɒn tiː viː] im Fernsehen *5.3*
one day [wʌn deɪ] eines Tages 6.3
only [ˈəʊnlɪ] nur *E1*
open [ˈəʊpən] öffnen; aufmachen *3R*, 4.3
operate on [ˈɒpəreɪt ɒn] operieren *4R*
opposite [ˈɒpəzɪt] Gegenteil *5R*
opposite [ˈɒpəzɪt] gegenüber 3.1
or [ɔː] oder 1.3
orange [ˈɒrɪndʒ] Orange; Apfelsine 1.2
organise [ˈɔːgənaɪz] organisieren *5.1*
other [ˈʌðə] anderer/andere/anderes *E2*
our [ˈaʊə] unser/unsere 4.1
outback [ˈaʊtbæk] Busch; Wüste *4R*
owner [ˈəʊnə] Inhaber/Inhaberin *3R*

P

pack [pæk] packen; einpacken *6R*
painting [ˈpeɪntɪŋ] Bild; Gemälde *E2*
park [pɑːk] Park S
part [pɑːt] Teil *E2*
partner [ˈpɑːtnə] Partner 3.3
party [ˈpɑːtɪ] Party; Fest; Feier 5.1
pass [pɑːs] reichen 6.2
past tense [pɑːst tens] Vergangenheitsform *6.2*
patient [ˈpeɪʃnt] Patient/Patientin *4R*
pen [pen] Stift; Füller 3.2
people [ˈpiːpl] Leute; Menschen *4.1*
person [ˈpɜːsn] Person 2.2
phone [fəʊn] Telefon 1.3: **on the phone** am Telefon; am Apparat *2.2*
photo [ˈfəʊtəʊ] Foto 2.1
photo album [ˈfəʊtəʊ ˈælbəm] Fotoalbum *6.2*
picnic [ˈpɪknɪk] Picknick 6.2
pizzeria [pɪzəˈrɪə] Pizzeria *3R*
place [pleɪs] Ort; Platz 2.3
plan [plæn] Plan *4.1*
plane [pleɪn] Flugzeug 4.3
play [pleɪ] spielen 3.3
please [pliːz] bitte 1.2
policemen [pəˈliːsmən] Polizisten *E1*
population [ˌpɒpjʊˈleɪʃn] Bevölkerung *1.1*
positive [ˈpɒzətɪv] positiv, bejahend *4.2*
post office [ˈpəʊstɒfɪs] Postamt 3.1
postcard [ˈpəʊstkɑːd] Postkarte *2R*, 3.1
pound [paʊnd] Pfund 3.1
present [ˈpreznt] Geschenk *6.2*
Prime Minister [praɪˈmɪnɪstə] Premierminister *E1*
prince [prɪns] Prinz *2R*
princess [prɪnˈses] Prinzessin *2R*
problem [ˈprɒbləm] Problem 2.1
profile [ˈprəʊfaɪl] Kurzbiographie *6.1*
pub [pʌb] Gaststätte; Kneipe; Wirtschaft; Lokal 2.3
pullover [ˈpʊləʊvə] Pullover *2R*
punt [pʌnt] Stocherkahn *5.1*
put [pʊt] tun; stellen; setzen; legen 4R

Q

queen [kwiːn] Königin *2R*
quiet [ˈkwaɪət] ruhig; leise 6.2

R

radio [ˈreɪdɪəʊ] Radio; Rundfunk *E1*
radio station [ˈreɪdɪəʊ steɪʃn] Rundfunktstation *4.2*
railway(s) [ˈreɪlweɪz] Eisenbahn(en) *3.2*
rain [reɪn] Regen *E2*, 5.2
rain [reɪn] regnen 5.2
read [riːd] lesen 4.1
really [ˈrɪəlɪ] wirklich; tatsächlich 2.1
receptionist [rɪˈsepʃənɪst] Person am Empfang *6.3*
red [red] rot *E2*
relaxing [rɪˈlæksɪŋ] entspannend; erholsam *6.2*
remember [rɪˈmembə] sich erinnern *4.3*: **I can't remember** ich kann mich nicht erinnern 5R
reporter [rɪˈpɔːtə] Reporter *6.1*
restaurant [ˈrestrɒnt] Restaurant 2.3
right [raɪt] rechts 3.1
right [raɪt] richtig *5.1*
river [ˈrɪvə] Fluß 5.I
road [rəʊd] Straße *3.1*
rock [rɒk] Fels *E2*
Royal Family [ˈrɔɪəl ˈfæməlɪ] Königliche Familie *5.1*

S

's (= is) [z] ist 1.3
's got/has got [həz/hæz gɒt] hat 2.3
same [seɪm] selber/selbe/selbes *E3*
sand [sænd] Sand *E2*
sandwich [ˈsænwɪdʒ] Sandwich; belegtes Brot S
Saturday [ˈsætədɪ] Samstag 3.3
saw [sɔː] sah(en/-st/-t) 5.3
say [seɪ] sagen 4.1
school [skuːl] Schule 5.3
sea [siː] Meer 6.I: **by the sea** am Meer 6.I
seat [siːt] (Sitz-)Platz; Sitz 1.2
second [ˈsekənd] zweiter/zweite/zweites *5.2*
see [siː] sehen *E1*
see [siː] sehen; besichtigen 4.3
send [send] schicken; senden 6.2
sentence [ˈsentəns] Satz 4R
service [ˈsɜːvɪs] Bedienung *6.3*
settling in [ˈsetlɪŋ ɪn] sich einleben *2.1*
she [ʃɪ/ʃiː] sie 1.3
shop [ʃɒp] Laden; Geschäft 2.3
shopkeeper [ˈʃɒpkiːpə] Ladeninhaber *3.1*
shopping centre [ˈʃɒpɪŋ ˈsentə] Einkaufszentrum *5R*
side [saɪd] Seite *E3*

sightseeing ['saɪtˌsiːɪŋ] Besichtigungen *5.1*
sister ['sɪstə] Schwester 2.2
sit [sɪt] sitzen *6R*
skateboard ['skeɪtbɔːd] Skateboard *5.3*
sky [skaɪ] Himmel *E1*
small [smɔːl] klein 6.1
small talk ['smɔːl tɔːk] Small Talk; Plauderei *4.2*
smile [smaɪl] Lächeln *6.1*
smile [smaɪl] lächeln *E2*, 6.2
so [səʊ] so *E1*
so [səʊ] also 3.3
so long [səʊ lɒŋ] tschüs; bis bald *1R*
sometimes ['sʌmtaɪmz] manchmal 4.2
son [sʌn] Sohn 2.2
sorry ['sɒrɪ] Entschuldigung; Verzeihung; es tut mir leid 2R
souvenir [suːvə'nɪə] Souvenir 6.2
speak [spiːk] sprechen 4.1
spell [spel] buchstabieren 6.3
sport [spɔːt] Sport; Sportart 3.3
sports centre [spɔːts 'sentə] Sportzentrum 3.3
squash [skwɒʃ] Squash S
stamp [stæmp] Briefmarke 3.1
start [stɑːt] anfangen; beginnen 4.2
start work [stɑːt wɜːk] zu arbeiten anfangen 4.2
state [steɪt] Staat; staatlich 3.2
station ['steɪʃn] Bahnhof *4.3*
stay [steɪ] bleiben; übernachten 5.2
steak [steɪk] Steak S
stereo set ['sterɪəʊ set] Stereoanlage *E1*
still [stɪl] (immer) noch *3R*
story ['stɔːrɪ] Geschichte *5.1*
stranger ['streɪndʒə]: **I'm a stranger here** ich bin hier fremd; ich bin nicht von hier 3R
street [striːt] Straße *E1*, 3.1
student ['stjuːdənt] Student/Studentin 2.2
suddenly ['sʌdnlɪ] plötzlich 5.1
summer ['sʌmə] Sommer 2.2
sun [sʌn] Sonne *E2*
Sunday ['sʌndɪ] Sonntag 3.3
super ['suːpə] super; klasse *2R*
supermarket ['suːpəmɑːkɪt] Supermarkt 3R
sweatshirt ['swetʃɜːt] Sweatshirt S
Swedish ['swiːdɪʃ] schwedisch *4.2*
sweet [swiːt] süß *5R*
swimming pool ['swɪmɪŋ puːl] Schwimmbad; Schwimmbecken 2R
Switzerland ['swɪtsələnd] die Schweiz 1.3
symbol ['sɪmbl] Symbol *E2*

T

T-shirt ['tiːʃɜːt] T-Shirt S
table ['teɪbl] Tabelle *6.2*
take [teɪk] (mit)nehmen 6.2
take a photo [teɪk ə 'fəʊtəʊ] ein Foto machen 6.2
take off ['teɪk ɒf] Start *E1*
talk to [tɔːk tʊ] sprechen mit *6.1*
taxi ['tæksɪ] Taxi 6.3
tea [tiː] Tee 1.2
tea cosy ['tiː kəʊzɪ] Teewärmer *6.2*
teacher ['tiːtʃə] Lehrer/Lehrerin 4R
teenager ['tiːneɪdʒə] Teenager *1R*
telephone ['telɪfəʊn] Telefon 2.1
television ['telɪvɪʒn] Fernsehgerät; Fernseher 2.1
tell [tel] erzählen; sagen *E2*, 5R
tennis ['tenɪs] Tennis S
thank [θæŋk] danken *6.3*
thank you ['θæŋk jʊ] danke (schön) 1.2
thank you very much [θæŋk jʊ verɪ 'mʌtʃ] vielen herzlichen Dank 3.1
thanks [θæŋks] danke 1.1
that [ðət] das 2R
that's alright [ðæts ɔːl'raɪt] schon gut; das macht nichts 2R
the [ðə] der; die; das 1.3
theatre ['θɪətə] Theater *E3*
their [ðeə] ihr 4.1
them [ðem] sie; ihnen *3.2*, 6.1
then [ðen] dann *3R*, 5.2
there [ðeə] da; dort 4.3
there are [ðeə ɑː] es gibt *E2*
there is [ðeə ɪz] es gibt; da ist *5R*
they [ðeɪ] sie 2.1
thing [θɪŋ] Ding *6R*
think [θɪŋk] denken; glauben 3R
think of [θɪŋk əv] halten von 6.1
this [ðɪs] dies; das 1.1
this is [ðɪs ɪz] dies ist 1.1
Thursday ['θɜːzdɪ] Donnerstag 3.3
time [taɪm] Zeit 3.3
tired ['taɪəd] müde 4.2
to [tʊ/tuː] zu 2.3
toast [təʊst] Toast *4.2*
too [tuː] auch 1.3
too [tuː] zu 4.3
tour [tʊə] Tour; Rundfahrt; Rundreise 5.3
tourist ['tʊərɪst] Tourist 4.3
tourist information (office) ['tʊərɪst ɪnfə'meɪʃn 'ɒfɪs] Fremdenverkehrsbüro 4.3
town [taʊn] Stadt *1.2*
town hall [taʊn hɔːl] Rathaus *6.3*
tradition [trə'dɪʃn] Tradition *6R*
train [treɪn] Zug 4.3
train [treɪn] eine Ausbildung machen; ausgebildet werden 6.1
transport ['trænspɔːt] Transport, Verkehr *4.3*
travel ['trævl] reisen; fahren 5.2
trip [trɪp] Reise; Ausflug 6.3
try [traɪ] versuchen *E2*
Tuesday ['tjuːzdɪ] Dienstag 3.3
turn [tɜːn] (ein-/ab-)biegen; drehen; wenden 3.1
turn right [tɜːn raɪt] biegen Sie/bieg rechts ein 3.1
typical ['tɪpɪkl] typisch *4R*

U

umbrella [ʌm'brelə] Regenschirm *6.2*
understand [ʌndə'stænd] verstehen 2R
university [juːnɪ'vɜːsətɪ] Universität *5.1*
us [ʌs] uns *E2*, 6.1
usually ['juːʒəlɪ] gewöhnlich; normalerweise 3.3

V

vegetation [vedʒɪ'teɪʃn] Vegetation *E2*
very ['verɪ] sehr 2.3
video ['vɪdɪəʊ] Video S
video camera ['vɪdɪəʊ 'kæmrə] Videokamera 2.1
village ['vɪlɪdʒ] Dorf 6.I
visit ['vɪzɪt] besuchen 5.2

W

walk [wɔ:k] laufen; zu Fuß gehen 4.3
want to [wɒnt tə] wollen *6.1*
was [wɒs] war 5.1
was/were born [wɒz/wɜ: bɔ:n] bin/ist/sind/bist/seid geboren 6.1
watch [wɒtʃ] zusehen *6R*
water ['wɔ:tə] Wasser 5.1
we [wɪ/wi:] wir 2.1
weather ['weðə] Wetter 4.1
Wednesday ['wenzdɪ] Mittwoch 3.3
week [wi:k] Woche 3.3
weekend [wi:k'end] Wochenende 3.3
welcome ['welkəm]: **you're welcome** bitte sehr; nichts zu danken; gern geschehen 1.3
welcome to ['welkəm tə] willkommen in 1.2
well [wel] nun (ja); also 4.3
well [wel] gesund 5.1: **wasn't very well** fühlte sich nicht gut 5.1
went [went] ging(en/-est/-et); fuhr(en/-st/-t) 5.3
were [wɜ:] warst; wart; waren 5.1
what? [wɒt] was? 1.3
what time is it? [wɒt taɪm ɪz ɪt] wie spät ist es?; wieviel Uhr ist es? 3.2
what time? [wɒt taɪm] um wieviel Uhr?; wann? 4.3
what's ... in English? [wɒts ... ɪn 'ɪŋglɪʃ] was bedeutet ... auf englisch? 1R
what's ... like? [wɒts ... laɪk] wie ist ...? 2.3
what's his name? [wɒts hɪz neɪm] wie heißt er?; wie ist sein Name? 2.2
what's your phone number? [wɒts jɔ: fəʊn 'nʌmbə] wie ist Deine/Ihre Telefonnummer? 1.3
when? [wen] wann? 3.3
where? [weə] wo? 1.3
where are you from? ['weərə ju: frɒm] wo sind Sie / bist du her?; woher sind Sie / bist du? 1.3
whisky ['wɪskɪ] Whisky 3.2
who? [hu:] wer? 2.2
who ... with? [hu: wɪð] mit wem? 5.3
why? [waɪ] warum? 3.3
wife [waɪf] Ehefrau 2.2
win [wɪn] gewinnen *E1*
windmill ['wɪnmɪl] Windmühle *6.1*
winter ['wɪntə] Winter 4.1
with [wɪð] mit *E1*, 4.1
woman ['wʊmən] Frau *E2*
wonderful ['wʌndəfʊl] wunderbar *E3*
word [wɜ:d] Wort 4R
work [wɜ:k] Arbeit 6.1
work [wɜ:k] arbeiten *3.1*, 3.2: **start work** zu arbeiten anfangen 4.2
would like ('d like) [wʊd laɪk] möchten 4.3
write [raɪt] schreiben *2R*, 4.1
wrong number [rɒŋ 'nʌmbə] falsch verbunden 2R

Y

year [jɪə] Jahr 5.2
yes [jes] ja 1.2
yesterday ['jestədɪ] gestern 5.1
you [jʊ/ju:] du; ihr; Sie 1.1
you must be [ju: məst bi:] Sie müssen/du mußt ... sein 1.2
you're welcome [jɔ: 'welkəm] bitte sehr; nichts zu danken; gerne geschehen 1.3
your [jɔ:] dein; ihr; Ihr 1.3

People's names

Women

Anita [ə'ni:tə]
Barbara ['bɑ:bərə]
Catherine ['kæθərɪn]
Elizabeth [ɪ'lɪzəbəθ]
Helen ['helɪn]
Janice [dʒænɪs]
Jessica ['dʒesɪkə]
Joanna [dʒəʊ'ænə]
Karen [kə'ren]
Margaret ['mɑ:gərɪt]
Mary ['meərɪ]
Peggy ['pegɪ]
Sally [sælɪ]
Samantha [sə'mænθə]
Sarah ['seərə]
Susan ['su:zn]
Tina ['ti:nə]
Vanessa [və'nesə]

Men

Alan ['ælən]
Andrew ['ændru:]
Barry ['bærɪ]
Bill [bɪl]
Chris ['krɪs]
Danny [dænɪ]
David ['deɪvɪd]
Dennis ['denɪs]
Glenn [glen]
Henry ['henrɪ]
Humphrey ['hʌmfrɪ]
James [dʒeɪmz]
Jonathan ['dʒɒnəθən]
Mark [mɑ:k]
Nick [nɪk]
Norman ['nɔ:mən]
Paul [pɔ:l]
Peter ['pi:tə]
Robert ['rɒbət]
Stanley ['stænlɪ]
Terry ['terɪ]
Tom [tɒm]
Victor [vɪktə]

Families

Biggs [bɪgz]
Brent [brent]
Brown [braʊn]
Cook [kʊk]
Denton ['dentən]
Jones [dʒəʊnz]
Keenan [ki:nən]
Lowen ['ləʊən]
Penny [penɪ]
Thomas ['tɒməs]
Williams ['wɪljəmz]
Wilson ['wɪlsn]

Alice Springs ['ælɪs sprɪŋz]	Kleinstadt in Mittelaustralien
America [ə'merɪkə]	Amerika
Australia [ɒs'treɪlɪə]	Australien
Ayers Rock [eəz rɒk]	großer Felsen in Mittelaustralien
Bath [bɑ:θ]	Stadt im Südwesten Englands
Berlin [bɜ:'lɪn]	Hauptstadt der Bundesrepublik Deutschland
Big Ben [bɪg ben]	*(Turmuhr am Parlamentsgebäude)*
Bristol [brɪstl]	Hafenstadt in Südwestengland
British Museum ['brɪtɪʃ mju:'zɪəm]	Britisches Museum
Buckingham Palace ['bʌkɪŋəm 'pælɪs]	Buckingham-Palast *(Sitz der Königin)*
Burnham Market [bɜ:nəm mɑ:kɪt]	Kleinstadt in Norfolk
Cam [kæm]	Fluß durch Cambridge
Cambridge [kæmbrɪdʒ]	Universitätsstadt im Südosten Englands
Canada ['kænədə]	Kanada
Cardiff ['kɑ:dɪf]	Hafenstadt in Wales
Chester ['tʃestə]	Stadt in Mittelengland
Colchester ['kəʊltʃɪstə]	Stadt im Südosten Englands
Docklands ['dɒklənz]	*(zum Geschäftsviertel entwickeltes ehemaliges Hafengebiet)*
Downing Street [daʊnɪŋ stri:t]	Adresse des Premier Ministers
Duluth [də'lu:θ]	amerik. Stadt am Oberen See
Dundee [dʌn'di:]	Stadt in Schottland
Edinburgh ['edɪnbərə]	Großstadt in Schottland
England ['ɪŋglənd]	England
Europe ['jʊərəp]	Europa
Glasgow ['glɑ:zgəʊ]	Stadt in Schottland
Houses of Parliament ['haʊzɪz əv 'pɑ:ləmənt]	*(Parlamentsgebäude)*
Hunstanton [hʌn'stæntən]	Küstenstadt in Norfolk
Hyde Park [haɪd pɑ:k]	große Parkanlage in London
India ['ɪndɪə]	Indien
Italy ['ɪtəlɪ]	Italien
Japan [dʒə'pæn]	Japan
King's Lynn ['kɪŋz lɪn]	Stadt in Norfolk
Lake District ['leɪk dɪstrɪkt]	Seen- u. Erholungsgebiet in Nordengland (Cumbria)
Liverpool ['lɪvəpu:l]	Hafenstadt im Nordwesten Englands
London ['lʌndən]	Hauptstadt Großbritanniens
London Transport Museum [lʌndən træns'pɔ:t mju:'zɪəm]	Verkehrsmuseum in London
Manchester ['mæntʃɪstə]	Industriestadt im Nordwesten Englands
Madame Tussaud's ['mædəm tə'sɔ:dz]	Wachsfigurenkabinett in London
Montreal [mɒntrɪ'ɔ:l]	Großstadt in Kanada
Munich ['mju:nɪk]	München
New York [nju: 'jɔ:k]	Großstadt an der Nordostküste der USA
Newcastle ['nju:kɑ:sl]	Stadt in Nordengland
Niagara Falls [naɪ'ægərə fɔ:lz]	große Wasserfälle zwischen Ontario- und Eriesee
Norfolk ['nɔ:fək]	Grafschaft im Südosten Englands
Norwich ['nɒrɪdʒ]	größte Stadt in Norfolk
Olga National Park ['ɒlgə næʃənl pɑ:k]	Nationalpark in Australien
Osaka ['ɔ:sɑkə]	Großstadt in Japan
Ottawa ['ɒtəwə]	Hauptstadt von Kanada
Ouse [u:z]	Fluß in Norfolk
Oxford Street ['ɒksfəd stri:t]	Einkaufsstraße in London
Pakistan [pɑ:kɪ'stɑ:n]	Pakistan
Piccadilly Circus [pɪkə'dɪlɪ 'sɜ:kəs]	*(Platz in London mit Erosstatue)*
Prague [prɑ:g]	Hauptstadt der tschechischen Republik
Princes Street [prɪnsɪz stri:t]	Hauptstraße in Edinburgh
Quebec [kwɪ'bek]	Stadt und Provinz in Kanada
San Francisco [ˌsæn fræn'sɪskəʊ]	Stadt in Kalifornien
Scotland ['skɒtlənd]	Schottland
Sweden ['swi:dn]	Schweden
Switzerland ['swɪtsələnd]	Schweiz
Toronto [tə'rɒntəʊ]	Stadt in Kanada
Tower of London ['taʊər əv 'lʌndən]	*(Londoner Burg, Turm von London)*
Trafalgar Square [trə'fælgə 'skweə]	*(Platz in London mit Nelsonsäule)*
Wales [weɪlz]	Wales
Wessex ['wesɪks]	Grafschaft in England
Wimbledon [wɪmbldən]	Kleinstadt bei London

STUDENT CHECK LIST

Anhand dieser Tabelle können Sie Ihre Lernfortschritte überprüfen. In der Spalte Situationen können Sie ablesen, was Sie mit dem erlernten Sprachmaterial tun, und welche Situationen Sie bewältigen können. Außerdem sehen Sie, welche Grammatik- und Wortschatzbereiche Sie bearbeiten und welche Laute in der Aussprache besonders geübt werden. In der Spalte rechts können Sie mit Haken (✔) und Datum kontrollieren, wie sich Ihre Kenntnisse von Step zu Step aufbauen.

Unit	Step	Situationen	Grammatik / Wortschatz / Aussprache	gelernt
1 *Arrival*	1	Begrüßen und Vorstellen: *Hello / How are you? / I'm ... / This is ... / Nice to meet you.*	Verb *be*: Aussagen/Fragen mit *I/you.*	
	2	Einladungen: *Come in / Have a seat / A cup of tea? / Yes, please / Thank you / No, thanks.* Begrüßen: *You must be ... / Welcome to ...*	Fragen und Kurzantworten mit *are/am* Befehlsform des Verbs *a - an* Wortfeld: Speisen und Getränke	
	3	Über Herkunft sprechen: *Where are you from? / I'm from ...* Telefonnummern erfragen und geben Etwas überreichen: *Here's ...*	Verb *be*: Aussagen/Fragen/Kurzantworten mit *you/he/she.* Zahlen 1-10	
2 *Settling in*	1	Vorhandensein/Besitz ausdrücken: *Have they/you got ...? / I've got ...* Überraschung/Freude ausdrücken: *Really?/Good.*	*Have got*: Aussagen/Fragen/Kurzantworten Wortfeld: Gegenstände zu Hause Aussprache: [f] - [v]	
	2	Auskünfte über Familien(mitglieder) erfragen und geben: *Who's this? / It's / Have you got ...? / I've got ...* Zugehörigkeit ausdrücken	*'s*- und *of*-Genitiv; Possessivpronomen Verb *be*: Pluralformen; Fragewörter Wortfeld: Familienangehörige Aussprache: [iː] - [ɪ]	
	3	Fragen über einen Ort stellen: *What's ... like? / Has it got ...? / It's got ...* Vorschläge machen: *Let's ...*	*Has got*: Aussagen/Fragen/Kurzantworten Zahlen 11-20; Plural des Hauptworts Wortfeld: Gebäude/Einrichtungen Aussprache: [ə]	
3 *Getting about*	1	Nach dem Weg fragen: *Where's the nearest ...? / On the left/right / Turn ...* Nach dem Preis fragen: *How much is/ are ...? / (It's/They're) £...*	Zahlen 21-100; Geldbeträge Präpositionen des Ortes Befehlsform des Verbs Aussprache: [θ] - [s]	
	2	Fragen und sagen, was man mag: *I like ... / Do you like ...?* Fragen und sagen, wo man arbeitet. Uhrzeit erfragen/sagen: *What time is it? / It's ...*	Aussagen in der Gegenwart (ohne 3. Person) Fragen und Kurzantworten mit *do* Uhrzeit Aussprache: [e] - [æ]	
	3	Freizeitbeschäftigungen erfragen und beschreiben: *I (usually) ... / Do you ...? / Where/When/What ...?* Zeitangaben machen	Verneinung mit *don't* Die Wochentage Wortfeld: Sport und Spiel Aussprache: Satzmelodie bei Fragesätzen	

Unit	Step	Situationen	Grammatik / Wortschatz / Aussprache	gelernt
4 *People and plans*	1	Sagen, welche Sprachen man kann: *I speak/understand (a bit of) ...* Über Familienmitglieder erzählen	Gegenwart 3. Person Fragen/Kurzantworten mit *does* Aussprache: [tʃ] - [dʒ]	
	2	Tagesablauf beschreiben/erfragen Zeitangaben machen: *never/sometimes/ often/usually/always/ How often?*	Verneinung mit *doesn't* Stellung der Zeitadverbien Wortfeld: alltägliche Handlungen Aussprache: [əʊ] - [ɒ]	
	3	Wünsche angeben und erfragen: *I'd like to ... / Would you like to ...?* Öffnungs-/Ankunfts-/Abfahrtszeiten angeben und erfragen	Gegenwart: *Wh*-Fragen mit *does* Aussagen/Fragen mit *would like* Wortfeld: Verkehrsmittel Aussprache: [r]	
5 *Sightseeing*	1	Vergangenes berichten/erfragen Sagen, daß es einem nicht gut geht	Vergangenheit: Aussagen/Fragen/Kurzantworten mit *was/were* Aussprache: [w]	
	2	Vergangenes berichten/erfragen Begrüßungsformeln in einem Brief	Vergangenheitsformen regelmäßiger Verben Fragen und Kurzantworten mit *did*	
	3	Vergangenes berichten/erfragen	Vergangenheitsformen unregelmäßiger Verben Verneinung mit *didn't*	
6 *Goodbye*	1	Nach Alter und Geburtsjahr fragen: *How old are you? / When were you born? / In 19..* Persönliche Lebensgeschichte erzählen	Vergangenheit (Wiederholung) Zeitangaben der Vergangenheit Jahreszahlen Aussprache: [ə]	
	2	Um etwas bitten: *Can ...* Bei Tisch: *Can you pass me ...? / I'd like ... / Here you are.*	Fragen mit *can* und *have got* Objektpronomen Adjektive Aussprache: [s] - [z]	
	3	Buchstabieren: *Can you spell that, please? / Yes, it's ...* Danken und sich verabschieden: *Thanks for everything. / We really enjoyed it. Have a good trip. / It was lovely to ...*	*must* Das Alphabet Aussprache: Satzmelodie in Aussagesätzen	

Acknowledgements

We are grateful to the following for permission to reproduce copyright material:

Lyrics:

Songs *By Train* (page **76**) and *Number Seven* (page **42**) from *Cloudsongs* by Brian Abbs, Longman Group UK Ltd., Harlow
Song *In the Summer* (page **110**) by Ken Wilson from *Mainline Beginners A* by Louis Alexander, Longman Group UK Ltd. Harlow

Illustrations:

Jürgen Bartz, München: page **6**
London Tourist Board and Convention Bureau, London: page **79** (bottom middle)
The Post Office, London: page **44** (top right)

Photographs:

Adidas AG, Public Relations & Presse Deutschland, Herzogenaurach: page **4** (No.7)
Australian Tourist Commission, Frankfurt: pp. **60** (bottom left), **75**, **77** (left)
Barnaby's Picture Library, London: pp. **9** (middle), **44** (bottom), **79** (top right), **109**
Bavaria-Verlag Bildagentur GmbH, München-Gauting: pp. **31** (Nägele), **43** (Kossmehl), **111** (bottom right: Photobank)
Bayerischer Rundfunk, Pressestelle, München: page **60** (bottom right)
Borough Council of King's Lynn and West Norfolk, Mr Pratley, King's Lynn: pp. **5** (No. 11), **10**, **39**, **45** (middle right, bottom left), **53**, **61** (top right), **93-95**
Reinhard Brendli, München: page **58** (Nos. 1-4)
British Tourist Authority, London: pp. **23**, **58** (No. 6), **68**, **78** (top, bottom left), **79** (middle left)
Dr. Sonia Brough, Oxford: pp. **5** (No. 10), **78** (bottom right)
Camera Press, London: page **41** (top left: Albert Watson)
C.O.I., Central Office of Information, London: page **59** (left)
Susan Darrant, München: page **84** (bottom right)
City of Edinburgh District Council, PR and Tourism Dept., Edinburgh: page **111** (left)
Michael Hyde, Kendal, Cumbria: page **4** (No. 3)
IFA-Bilderteam GmbH, München-Taufkirchen: pp. **5** (No. 14: Heinz Koch)
Interfoto Pressebild-Agentur/Bildarchiv, München: pp. **4** (No. 8: Ksandr), **5** (No. 15: Ksandr), **77** (bottom right)
Nick Jones, Bath: page **4** (No. 2)
London Transport Museum: page **61** (top left, middle left/right, bottom)
Longman Group UK Ltd., Harlow, Essex; photography by Mr Trevor Clifford; Research and Art Directing by Hilary Fletcher and Ann Hazelwood, special thanks to Kevin and Lyn Disley and Alan Fletcher: pp. **6-8**, **9** (top/bottom) **11**, **25-27**, **44** (centre), **45** (top), **60** (centre), **95** (middle left), **98**
McDonalds Deutschland Inc., München: page **5** (No. 13)
Mauritius Bildagentur GmbH, Mittenwald: **pp.** 4 (No. 4: U. Kerth), **58** (No. 5: Mollenhauer), **79** (top left: ACE)
Wolfgang Pichler, Hallein/Österreich: page **5** (No. 9)
Barbara Suhr, Kiel: page **4** (No.1)
U.S. Information Service, DES/Photos, Embassy of the United States of America, Bonn: page **35** (bottom right)
Angelika Wagner, München: pp. **4** (No. 5), **5** (No. 12)
Zero Grafik & Design GmbH, München: page **4** (No. 6)

Cover photograph by Andy Williams Photolibrary, Guildford, Surrey

We should be very grateful for any information which might assist us in tracing the copyright owners of sources which w have been unable to acknowledge.